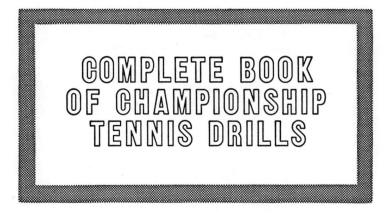

COMPLETE BOOK
OF CHAMPIONSHIP
TENNIS DRILLS

COMPLETE BOOK OF CHAMPIONSHIP TENNIS DRILLS

Bill Murphy

Parker Publishing Company, Inc.
West Nyack, New York

© 1975 by

Parker Publishing Company, Inc.
West Nyack, New York

Library of Congress Cataloging in Publication Data

Murphy; Bill,
　　Complete book of championship tennis drills.

　　1.　Tennis.　I.　Title.
GV995.M82　　796.34'22　　　　　　74-23175
ISBN 0-13-156026-3

Printed in the United States of America

Foreword

When I was asked to look over the manuscript for this book, my first thought was that the book would differ very little from the many fine works on tennis that have been published in such abundance in recent years. After reading the manuscript, however, I must confess that I became intrigued with its contents, realizing that here is a book that is sorely needed by players, teachers, and coaches alike. Why, I wondered, was it not written sooner?

I have known the author for many years and I am thoroughly familiar with his playing ability and his teaching and coaching ability. His record first as a high school coach and then as a college coach at the University of Michigan and the University of Arizona is an outstanding one. He has drawn on this coaching experience and on experience gained in more than 15 years of club teaching to compile the material in this book. Here he presents, in simple diagrams and easily understood text, practically every effective drill used to improve tennis skills. Many of the drills will be familiar to you if you are an experienced player or coach; yet, regardless of your background in the game, you will find something new and helpful here. Whether you be player, teacher, or coach, within these pages you will find a wealth of information on how to improve tennis skills.

Dale A. Lewis

Head Tennis Coach
University of Miami
Coral Gables, Florida

How This Book Will Help You

This book adds a new dimension to tennis instruction in that it goes beyond stroke techniques and tactics by providing a thorough program of individual and team drills that will increase the effectiveness of practice sessions. Whatever the age level of a player, whatever the degree of his experience or background in the game, the contents of this book provide the basis for improving his development of skills up to the level of championship play.

Drills contribute to the learning process in several ways. They provide a means for a player to make repeated attempts at a skill or a stroke in a short period of time; they enable a teacher or coach to keep a large group of players active in a small area; and they permit all players in a group to benefit from corrective suggestions made by the coach to one player. In addition, they develop team spirit and morale and they add fun and variety to a program.

The constant repetition of trying a skill during a drill is the most effective way for a player to learn the skill. He needs competitive experience, but until he attains a high level of performance, he needs repeated practice in individual skills even more, because seldom does actual game participation provide sufficient repetition of the skill to enable him to learn it and to "nail it down" so that it becomes automatic. The constant repetition of trying a skill in practice, without the pressure of competition or the fear of losing a point, permits him to experiment, to try different ways of performing the skill, until he learns the best way of doing it. Through additional repetitions in practice, he reinforces the skill. He gains so much confidence in his ability to make a certain shot, for example, because he has made it so often in drills that simulate game situations, that when he gets the same shot in actual play, he has little fear of missing it, and usually makes it.

The use of drills is especially important in teaching, too, where often one teacher is assigned to teach 12, 14, or even more students on only one or two courts. A teacher confronted with this problem of "many players, few courts" simply must make use of drills that involve several players on one court even if only to keep everyone in the class active and busy.

Most successful coaches make extensive use of drills during team practice periods, also. Quite often a coach has his entire team or squad engage in a drill on only one or two courts. With the group thus concentrated within a small area, he can supervise the drill very closely. Because all players are within the sound of his voice, any corrections he makes to one player during the drill can be heard by all; thus they all benefit from the corrections.

Finally, certain drills can be helpful in adding fun and variety to a tennis program. When players get bored with the sometimes tedious and monotonous routine of practice, the use of selective drills that involve a friendly kind of competition or contest can provide them with a period of diversion; having thus "blown off some steam" for a while, they are more likely to resume serious drills with increased enthusiasm and intent.

The drills presented in the book are grouped according to strokes and are listed in the order of difficulty—those requiring the least skill precede those requiring greater skill. This grouping is intended to make it easy for the reader, whether he be a teacher, coach, or player, to quickly select a drill suitable to his needs. Although most of the drills are described and illustrated in terms of either a group situation or a coach-student situation, all, with the exception of those concerned with doubles techniques, can be used by only two players. One player can act as the coach, or feeder, while the other practices the skill.

Many of the drills have been given descriptive names that facilitate their use. Such terms as Three-Shot, Speedy-V, and Short Corner not only describe certain drills to a degree, but also aid in the recall of them once players have had some experience with them.

Players need be shown the drill only once—a demonstration by one unit is usually sufficient—and, because of its name, they can easily recall it. Much detailed explanation and demonstration is thus avoided, then, when a coach assigns players to work on a specific drill; he merely names the drill, the players recall it, and they begin to work on it.

The extent of the benefit of the drills program that follows will depend upon the degree of effort and work expended by the player. Here is presented a means of maximum skills development; a player need only to apply himself to regular and intensive practice in the drills to reach the championship level of play.

Bill Murphy

Table of Contents

III. VOLLEY DRILLS (*cont.*)

IV. LOB DRILLS   82

V. OVERHEAD SMASH DRILLS   85

VI. MISCELLANEOUS STROKE DRILLS   92

VII. DOUBLES DRILLS   108

VII. DOUBLES DRILLS *(cont.)*

VIII. DRILLS FOR CONDITIONING   138

IX. DRILLS AND FORMATIONS FOR BEGINNER'S STROKE INSTRUCTION   146

I

Ground Stroke Drills

Despite the current popularity of the "serve and rush to the net" type of game, the forehand and backhand ground strokes are still the cornerstones of a sound tennis game. Even a player who builds his game around the serve and volley is forced to play many ground strokes because, except when he is serving, he is able to attain his preferred position at the net only through a sound offensive use of ground strokes.

Beginners should learn to play tennis by first learning the ground strokes according to the following progressive steps:

1) the swing, including the grip and stance
2) hitting a dropped ball
3) hitting a tossed ball
4) running to hit a tossed ball
5) rallying

Several drills for beginners are presented in the chapter on Group Instruction (Chapter 9). Although these drills are described and illustrated in terms of a group or class, they can be modified easily and used by a beginning player working with a playing partner. These drills should be used until the beginner has progressed through the rallying stage.

Having learned to rally, the beginner is ready for more advanced drills which are designed to lead him beyond the beginner's level of play. Several such drills are presented in the following section.

1

THE LINE-OF-GOOD-POSITION IN THE BACK COURT

Beginning and low intermediate players should be taught the basic principle of position play: "As your opponent makes his shot, be ready and waiting on *the line-of-good-position*—the line that bisects the angle of his possible returns."

Applying this principle, a baseliner stands directly behind the center mark only when his opponent is hitting from *his* center mark (Figure 1-A). When the opponent is hitting from near the sides of the court (Figure 1-B and C), the baseliner should be about a step away from the center mark in the opposite direction from which his opponent is hitting.

In summary, what it amounts to is this: The baseliner moves to his left or right as his opponent moves to *his* left or right; he is in the center only when his opponent is in the center (Figure 1-D). Moving in this manner, the baseliner puts himself in the optimum position for returning his opponent's likely shots.

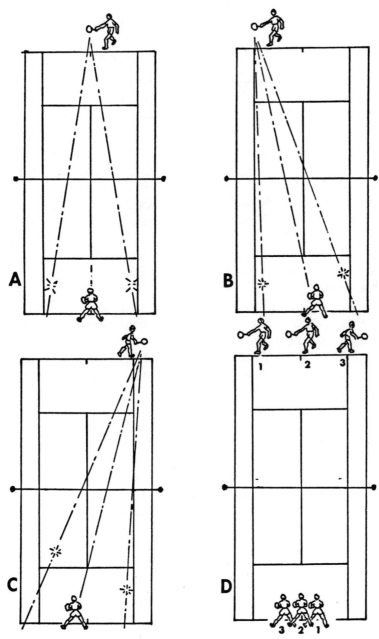

Figure 1

2

HOME BASE

Inexperienced players must learn to recover quickly by returning to "home base"—about three feet behind the center mark—after they have made a shot. Too often they move to the corner of the court to play a ball and just stand and watch the flight of the ball after they have hit it. They then wonder why they have so much difficulty in getting to their opponent's next shot!

A drill in which hitters are encouraged to return to home base helps them to be conscious of making a quick recovery after each shot (Figure 2).

The hitter stands at home base, in the center of the court about three feet behind the center mark. The coach or feeder stands in the opposite court, on the baseline, with an ample supply of balls. The coach drops-and-hits balls to the hitter, deliberately hitting the ball away from him, making him run to play it. Immediately after the hitter hits a ball, he returns to home base. The coach waits until the hitter has reached home base and then feeds another ball, again making the hitter run. Balls are not rallied; the coach feeds, the hitter runs, hits, and recovers to home base in preparation for the next feed.

One player hits at a time, while some additional group members wait in file off-court and others act as retrievers, keeping the coach supplied with balls. Players are rotated regularly so that all get hitting practice.

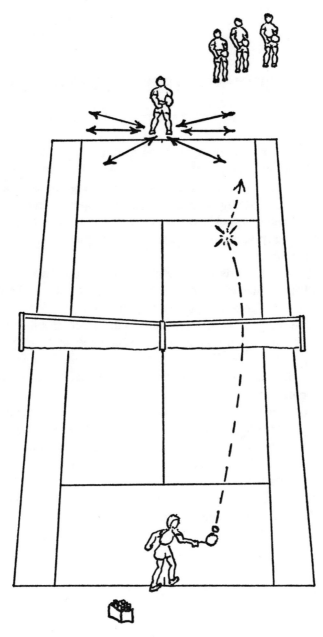

Figure 2

3
GROUND STROKE SCRAMBLE

In addition to learning to return to home base, players must learn to scramble all over the court. They must learn to be retrievers, to learn to play defense. Retrieving and scrambling require the ability to hit when off balance, to hit when running, and to change direction quickly when running. The Ground Stroke Scramble drill is a good one to give inexperienced players practice in these skills (Figure 3).

The hitter starts in the center of the court, two or three feet behind the center mark. A coach or feeder stands on the opposite baseline, with an ample supply of balls.

The coach drops-and-hits balls to the hitter, making him run all over the court. He mixes deep shots with short shots, easy hits with hard hits, low-flying balls with high-flying ones, hitting one ball quickly after another. The hitter scrambles quickly to try to return every ball.

After eight or nine hits, the scrambler moves to the end of the waiting line and another player becomes the scrambler. Other players, acting as retrievers, move into the waiting line at intervals and those who have already hit become retrievers.

As a variation of this drill, the coach can stand near the net and toss balls to the hitter, making him scramble to return the balls.

Both forehands and backhands or a combination of the two can be fed to the hitters.

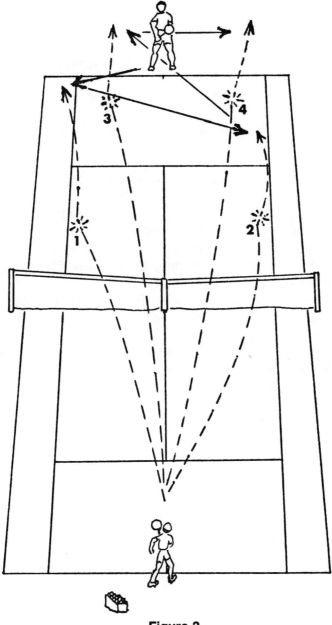

Figure 3

4
TWO-ON-ONE: GROUND STROKES

In actual competitive play, only occasionally does a player hit a ball that comes straight to him from a point directly in front of him. Most often he must play a ball that comes to him from a slight angle, from one corner of the court or the other. Only occasionally, too, does a player hit a ball straight ahead; most often he hits the ball at an angle, to one corner or the other.

Players should be given special practice in hitting angle shots so that they can learn the subtle changes in timing and wrist-action required to play these angled balls. A simple but effective drill for this is the Two-on-One (Figure 4).

Two players play on one baseline, one player plays on the opposite baseline. Players rally, with the two players trying to move the single player around the court by hitting cross-court and down the line. The single player scrambles along his baseline and returns all balls either cross-court or down the line, also.

Players are rotated regularly so that each gets practice rallying against two other players.

5
THREE-LANE

A drill called Three-Lane (Figure 5) is an effective one for giving players practice in hitting to the sides of the court and keeping the ball out of the middle.

Use rope or cord laid on the court surface and held in place at intervals with short pieces of masking tape to mark a center lane.

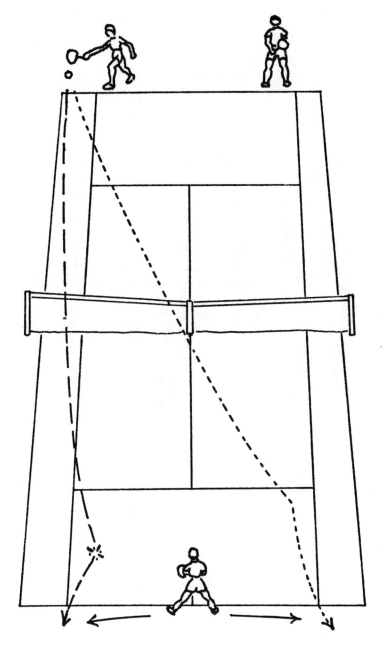

Figure 4

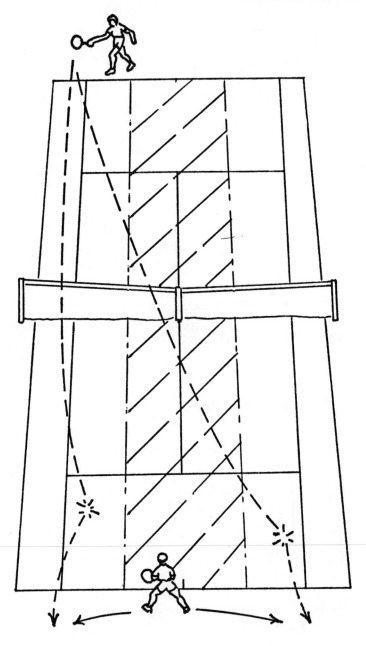

Figure 5

(Chalk or water-based tempera paint, which can be removed easily with a wet sponge, can also be used.) Make the center lane about 10 to 15 feet wide, depending upon the skill of the players.

Two players play singles. The serve is made into the regular service areas, but after the serve all balls must land in either of the outside lanes; the center lane, except for the serve, is out-of-bounds.

6

DEEP GAME

Players can be given special practice in hitting deep to an opponent's court by having them play the Deep Game (Figure 6).

Use rope, cord, or chalk to mark out deep areas that extend nine feet inside each baseline. Players play regulation singles, but all balls, with the exception of the serve, must land in the deep areas.

The Deep Game can be combined with Three-Lane (Figure 5). Mark out deep areas *and* a third lane; all balls (except the serve) must land in either of the deep outside lanes.

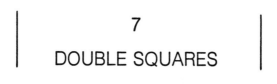

7

DOUBLE SQUARES

Advanced intermediate players can be given practice that will improve their ground stroke accuracy by having them play Double Squares (Figure 7).

Mark two deep areas inside each baseline (9′ squares) and two short areas inside each service line (4′ squares). Players then rally,

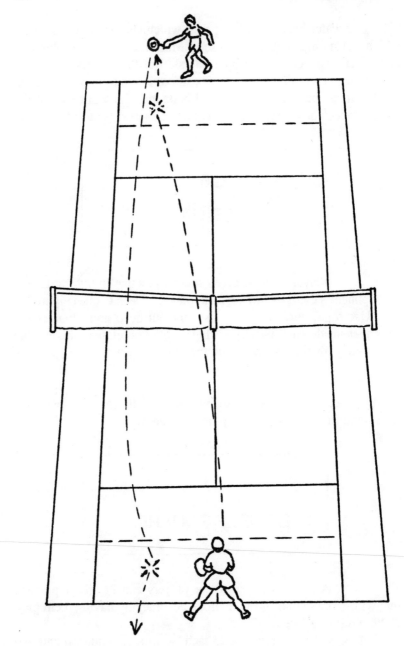

Figure 6

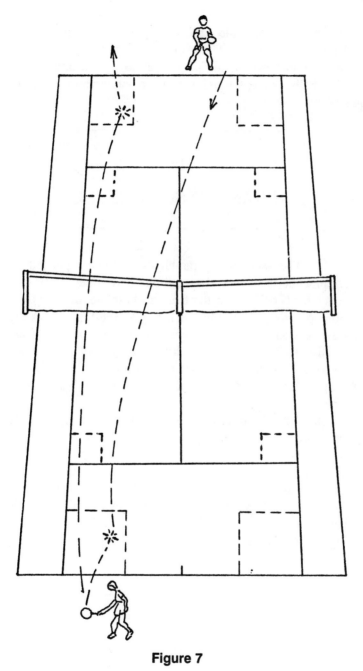

Figure 7

trying to hit every ball into either a deep or a short square. Any ball that lands outside either of the squares is "out."

Players can play modified singles using the double squares, too. All balls, except those served, must land in either of the squares.

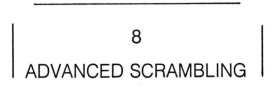

The back court scramble drill can be expanded to give players practice in advanced scrambling and volleying (Figure 8). The coach feeds balls to a hitter from the baseline, making the hitter scramble, by dropping-and-hitting (or by tossing) five or six balls in quick succession. After five or six deep feeds, the coach deliberately feeds a short ball so that the hitter must make an approach shot and an advance to the net. Either a short forehand or a short backhand can be fed to the hitter, depending upon which he most needs to practice.

As the hitter approaches the net, the coach drops-and-feeds several more balls, all in rapid succession, forcing the hitter to volley quickly.

The drill can be used with a group, also, with some players acting as retrievers while others wait in line behind the hitter. After one player has hit, he moves to the end of the waiting line and another player becomes the hitter. Retrievers are rotated into the waiting line so that they, too, can participate in the drill.

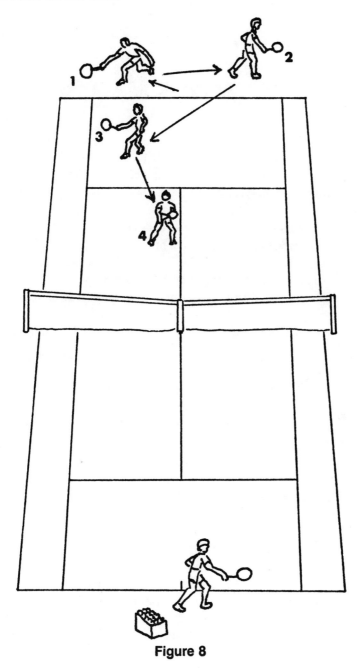

Figure 8

9
APPROACH SHOT TACTICS

Approach shots, both forehand (Figure 9) and backhand (Figure 10), generally should be hit deep and straight ahead. In approaching the net behind such a shot, a player has a shorter distance to run in order to be on the line-of-good-position (position's 1 in Figures 9 and 10) than he would have if he were to hit cross-court. If he *were* to hit cross-court, he would have to reach position 2 (in each diagram) to be on the line-of-good-position, and would have to run a greater distance to do so. Most likely, he would not be able to reach these positions in time to make a forceful volley.

10
APPROACH SHOT DRILLS

Players must learn to look for the short ball, to pounce on it when it comes, and to hit it forcefully and deep so that they can make a safe approach to the net. Specific practice in making the approach shot is necessary so that a player's response to it becomes almost automatic.

The forehand approach shot is usually a drive, with the ball being hit either flat or with a slight amount of top spin. Intermediate players should try to get to the ball quickly so that they can stop or at least slow down as they hit, in order to have good control over the stroke. In more advanced play, players usually hit the ball on the run, with their front foot in mid-air as they advance to the net.

Both of these techniques can be practiced by using the drill

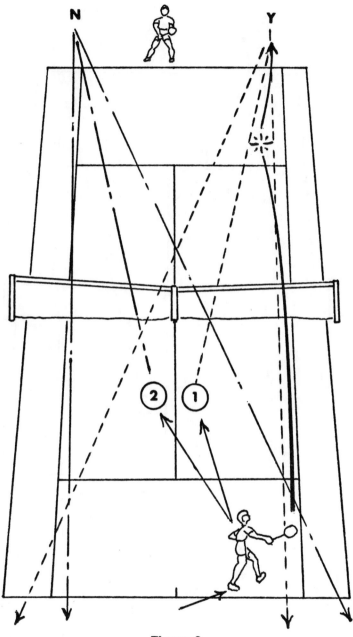

Figure 9

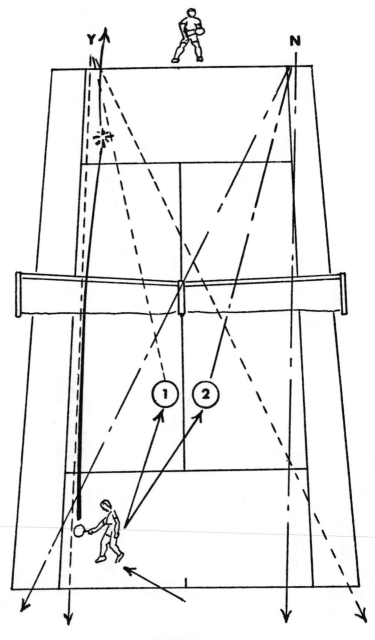

Figure 10

illustrated in Figure 11. A feeder stands on the baseline and deliberately feeds short balls to a hitter who stands at the center of the opposite baseline. As the short-ball approaches, the hitter runs to it, hits it deep and straight ahead, and then advances to the net behind the shot, being sure to be a little off-center on the line-of-good-position when he reaches the volleying position.

The backhand approach shot is hit straight ahead, also, and the hitter advances to the net behind it. Again he must be careful to be on the line-of-good-position when he reaches the volleying position. Because of the difficulty of combining a full swing with the necessary footwork, however, the ball is usually chipped or sliced rather than driven. The shot can be practiced as the forehand was, with a feeder deliberately feeding short balls to a hitter's backhand (Figure 12).

A group of players can practice the approach shots using file formations: the first player in a file hits, then moves to the end of the file. The next player in the file then hits and moves to the end of the file, and so on. Forehand shots, backhand shots, and a combination of forehands and backhands can be practiced (Figure 13).

11

APPROACH AND VOLLEY

After players have had some practice on approach shots they should begin to concentrate on making the volley following the approach. A drill similar to those used for approach shot practice is an effective one for this (Figure 14).

Again the coach deliberately feeds a short ball to the hitter, who makes a forcing shot and approaches the net. The drill does not stop at this point, however. Immediately after feeding the short ball, the coach moves to the corner of the court, to where the hitter will aim the approach shot. Then, as the hitter advances to the net after making his forcing shot, the coach drops another ball and feeds a

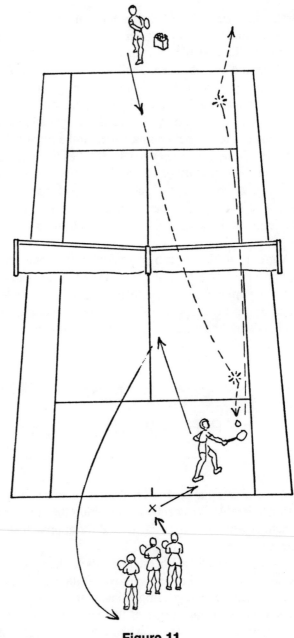

Figure 11

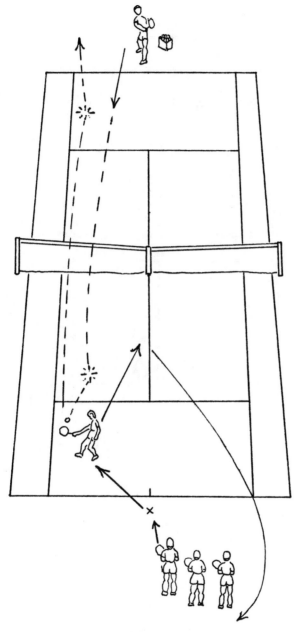

Figure 12

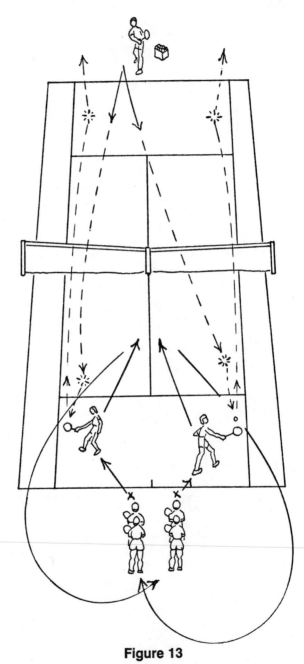

Figure 13

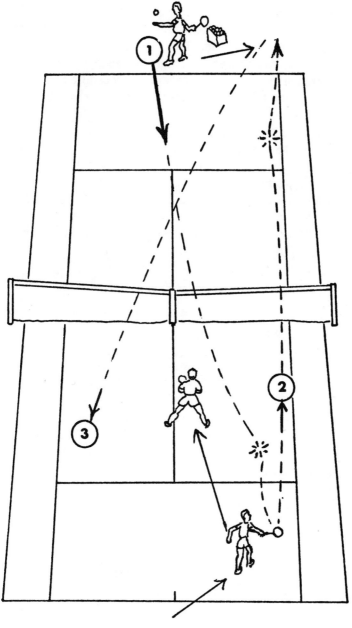

Figure 14

volley to the hitter. Two or three additional volleys can be fed
quickly to the hitter, who must not only volley the ball but must also
adjust his position to be on the line-of-good-position for each shot.

The coach can instruct the hitter on his approach shots, the
actual approach to the net, and the correct procedure for hopping to
the ready position as he approaches the net during the course of the
drill.

The backhand approach and volley can be practiced in a similar
manner, with the coach feeding short backhands to hitters and then
feeding volleys from the forehand corner (Figure 15).

In a group situation, some players act as retrievers while others
wait in line behind the hitter's baseline. After one player has hit, he
moves to the end of the waiting line and another player becomes the
hitter. Retrievers are rotated into the waiting line so that they can
practice the approach and volley, also.

12

PASSING SHOTS

Players can be introduced to passing shots through use
of a simple drill in which the coach stands in the volleying position
and feeds balls to a baseliner who then tries to pass the coach. Both
forehand and backhand passing shots can be practiced (Figures 16
and 17).

Inexperienced players will soon learn that a cross-court passing
shot must be aimed low and must be hit easier than the longer,
down-the-line passing shot, except when the volleyer is in bad position at the net.

When a hitter has begun to get some feel for direction and
speed in trying to pass a net man, the coach can try to volley the
attempted passing shots. Backcourters will quickly learn that they
often have to create an opening for a passing shot by being patient as
they move the net man around, trying to force him into a weak

Figure 15

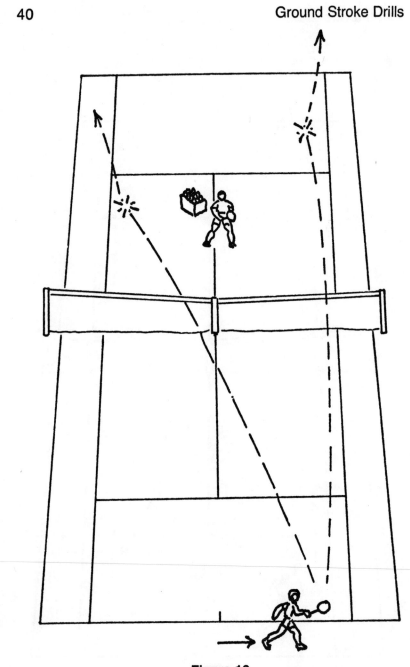

Figure 16

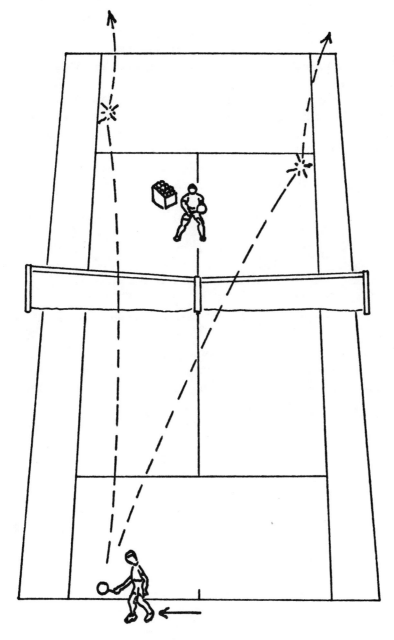

Figure 17

position and thus trying to force him into volleying short and weak. When the net man does volley short, the backcourt man should pounce on the ball, getting it at waist-level or higher, and hit it past the net man.

The coach can use the drill with a group of players, also. One player acts as the backcourter, other players wait in line behind him, and still others act as retrievers. The players are rotated regularly so that all get equal practice in passing a net man.

13

SHORT CORNER

In advanced play, a back-courter must be sly and cunning to pass a good volleyer. In addition to being able to hit hard, accurate drives, he must be able to hit low, sharp cross-court shots in order to create an opening through which he can hit his hard drives. The Short Corner drill (Figure 18) gives a player practice in these shots that create openings.

Two "short corners" are drawn in the court at the junction of the singles side lines and the service line. Two players take positions on a service line, with each standing about a foot to the side of the center line. A lone player plays deep in the opposite court.

Either player starts a rally. The single player hits ground strokes, aiming every shot for one of the short corners, trying to keep the ball low. The opposing players return all shots, hitting either volleys or half-volleys, and return to their starting positions after every hit. The ball is kept in play until a miss occurs, after which another rally is started.

Regular practice in hitting to the short corners teaches a player to "play cat and mouse" with a volleyer. He'll learn not to try for an outright winner too quickly; he'll learn to spar with a volleyer until an opening is created or until he gets a very easy shot which he can hit past the volleyer.

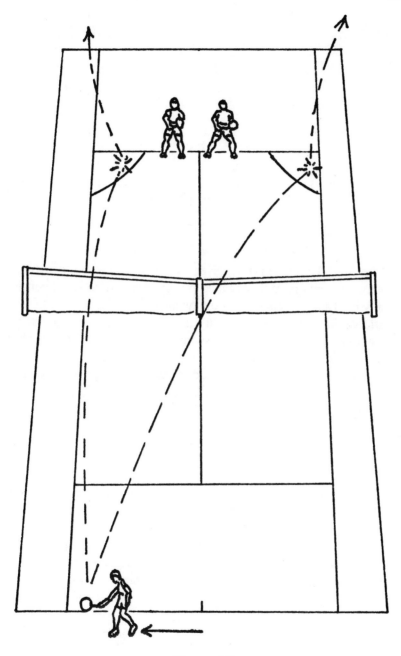

Figure 18

II

Serve Drills

The serve is the power-stroke of modern tennis. Almost without exception, highly ranked players are able to serve consistently hard and accurately. For many players, particularly those who start learning the serve incorrectly, it is a difficult stroke to master; once a player develops a faulty swing, he will have a difficult time making corrections in it.

In learning to serve, beginners should follow the sequence of:

1) the grip and stance,
2) the swing,
3) serving against a fence, and
4) serving on the court.

They should learn proper form first—while hitting easy balls—and then add speed, placement, and spin to develop a more advanced serve.

The serve is the only shot in tennis that a player can practice by himself. Once he has learned the basic mechanics of the swing, he need only go out on the court and, with as many tennis balls as he can gather, practice the serve, serving from both the right and left sides of the center mark.

14

SERVING FOR BEGINNERS

Most beginners should look upon the serve merely as a means of putting the ball in play. They can't, as a rule, serve hard and accurately. Usually they are more concerned about not serving a double fault than they are about using the serve as an offensive weapon.

The best place for a beginner to stand when serving from the right court is a foot or two to the right of the center mark.

If the server has good control over his serve, he should try to serve to the receiver's backhand (usually the weakest shot) into target area A (Figure 19). If the receiver "covers" his backhand, however, by standing toward the middle of the court, the serve should be made wide to target area B. In all cases, serves should be deep, landing very close to the service line.

If the serve is made deep to the receiver's backhand, the server should move quickly to the left—to about a foot left of the center mark, to await the return. This move will put the server to the left of the line-of-good-position. Seldom will he suffer any serious consequence from being off the line-of-good-position, however. Most often the receiver, because he is forced to play his weak backhand stroke, cannot place the ball with any speed to the opening on the server's right. Moreover, and most importantly, the server can then play most returns with his stronger forehand stroke.

When serving from the left court (Figure 20) the server should stand six or seven feet to the left of the center mark. From this position he can more easily serve to the receiver's backhand, forcing the receiver wide to his left, and thus opening the court for a sharp forehand cross-court shot. Again, however, if the receiver covers his backhand a great deal when receiving the serve, the server should frequently serve down the center of the court to target area B. Here, too, all serves should be made to land deep in the serving area.

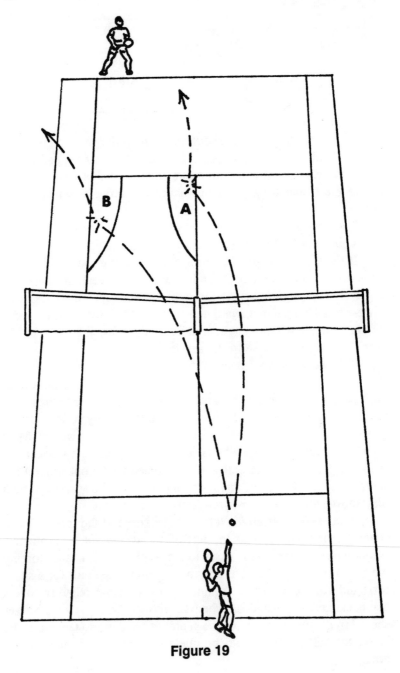

Figure 19

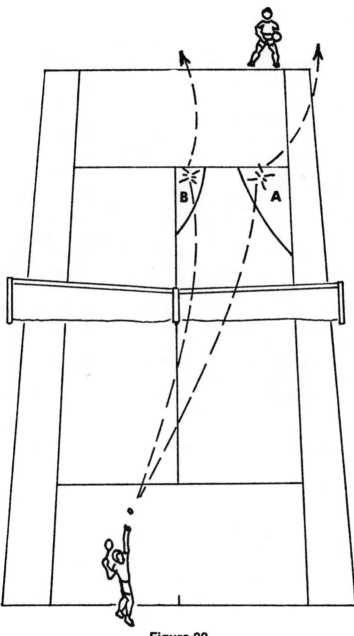

Figure 20

15

SERVE AND GO UP: SINGLES

Players can be introduced to the somewhat complex combination of moves of serving, going up to the net, and getting ready to deal with the return of the serve through a drill in which the coach actually serves while the players merely execute the serving motion and follow it with an advance to the net (Figure 21).

Several players form a file on one end of the court, with the first player in the file in the normal serving position. The coach, with an ample supply of balls at his disposal, stands in close proximity to the first player in the file. The coach serves while the leading player in the file simultaneously executes the serving motion. The player follows the coach's serve to the net, hops to the ready position (a well-balanced, ready-to-move position) immediately as the receiver of the serve begins his service-return stroke, and volleys the return. After the net-rusher has made the ready-hop and volley, he returns to the end of his file as the second player in the file moves into the serving position; the coach then serves for this second player.

If the class is large, several members can take turns returning the serves, rotating from the front to the rear of their files, also. All players, both servers and retrievers, are rotated regularly then so that all get equal practice in advancing to the net.

It is helpful, frequently, to precede this drill with a mass drill in which several players (five or six) spread out along the baseline and execute the serving motion simultaneously and advance to the net. The coach, meanwhile, stands on the opposite side of the net. As the group of players advances to the net, the coach simulates a return-of-serve stroke (either a forehand or a backhand swing), and the "servers" are given practice in hopping to the ready position just as the coach begins his swing.

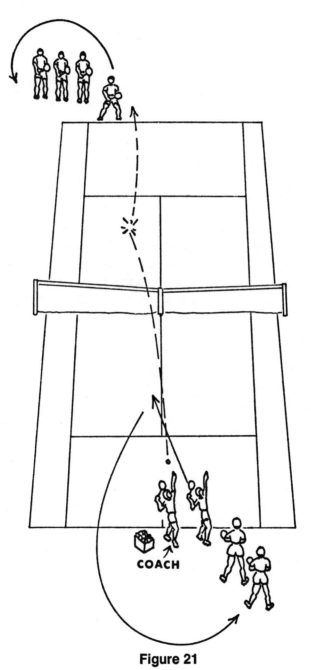

Figure 21

16

SERVE, GO UP, AND VOLLEY

Following the drill in which a player advances to the net behind the coach's serve, the player himself can serve and go up to the net, make the ready-hop, and volley the return-of-serve (Figure 22).

Here the server should be particularly careful about his line of approach, and his recovering quickly on the line-of-good-position in order to be ready for the receiver's second shot.

If the server serves wide to the receiver's forehand (line 1) so that the receiver is at A when returning the ball, the server's ready-hop should be made at position A on his side of the court (on the line-of-good-position).

If the first volley (line 3) is made to the receiver's backhand so that the receiver must play it from B, the server should quickly move to position B on his side of the court in order to be on the line-of-good-position.

The receiver should recover quickly after each of his shots, also. He will learn that generally his best return-of-serve is one that is hit low, to the server's feet, and slightly cross-court to the server's right. Such a return will minimize the angle the receiver will then have to cover for the second shot. Similar tactics apply when the server serves to the left court.

As in similar drills, a group of players can be accommodated if extra players form files on either side of the net, one file on the server's side and one on the receiver's side. Players then rotate in their files and from file to file, regularly, so that all get serving and receiving practice.

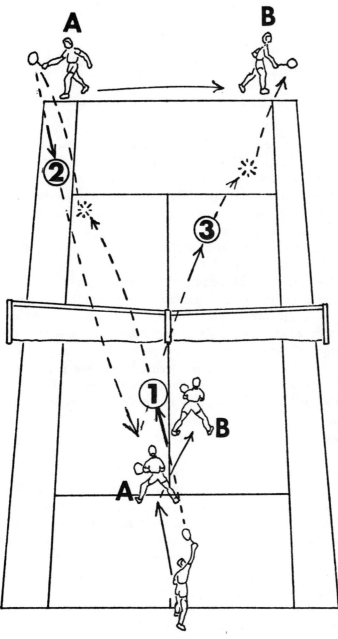

Figure 22

17

THREE-SHOT

Close analysis of match play at the Advanced Intermediate and Advanced levels of play indicates that most often a rally is terminated because of a miss of one of the following three shots: the return-of-serve, the first volley, or the shot following the first volley. Usually one of these shots is missed because a player overplays the ball. He tries to do too much with it, to make too good a shot. The Three-Shot drill is an effective one to provide practice in these three shots (Figure 23).

The squad is divided equally into two units, servers and receivers. One player in the serving unit serves, one in the receiving unit receives. These two players play a point, trying to complete the three-shot sequence. (The serve is not counted in the sequence; only the return-of-serve, the volley, and the next shot comprise the full sequence.) The players are not trying to win the point; they are merely trying to complete the three-shot sequence. When they do so, or if they fail to do so, they move off the court and two other players move on to attempt the sequence. Players continue to rotate, moving on and off the court after each attempt.

Emphasis during the drill should be placed on making the shots. It is helpful to have the players hit at three-quarter speed at first—they will be surprised how often they fail to complete the sequence even at this slow speed—and then gradually increase the speed until they are working at their normal competitive-play speed.

If four or six players are assigned to each of two or more courts, an entire squad can be accommodated. A contest between courts can be held, then, with the players on each court trying to beat those on the other courts. Each successful three-shot sequence is counted as one. The group of players completing the greatest number of three-shots sequences during the given time period is the winner.

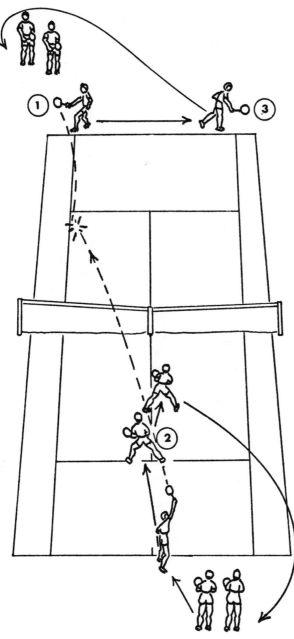

Figure 23

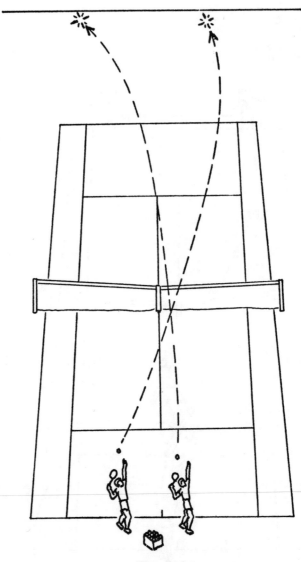

Figure 24

18

BOOMER SERVE

Despite the fact that he thinks he is serving as hard as he can, a player frequently does not use all the power he is capable of using. He does not always use all the latent power in his serving motion.

A drill in which a player tries to hit the base of the far fence with his serve is an effective one for convincing him that he is serving at less than maximum speed and strength (Figure 24).

Standing in normal serving position, he makes a normal serve except that he aims for the far fence rather than the service court. Most players, when they first try this, will find that their serves fall far short of the fence. Through continued attempts at hitting the fence, however, they will gradually add more and more power to their swings, and soon will be serving line-drives that reach the fence. They will be surprised at how much harder they must swing to do this, and will realize that they have not been using all of their power. They should be reminded to serve at full power when they return to practicing normal serves which they aim for specific targets within the service court.

III

Volley Drills

Before a player can achieve any degree of success in tennis, he must have reasonably sound ground strokes and a fairly good serve. These strokes alone, however, are not sufficient for him to advance into the above-average class of players. He must also learn to make the volleys in order to enter the championship class where the winning game is played mostly in the forecourt.

Beginners can learn to volley most quickly by first hitting tossed balls, then moving on to hitting driven balls. Some drills for the beginning volley are presented in the chapter on Group Teaching (Chapter 9). Once they have acquired some skill in simple beginning volleys through practice in these drills, beginners are ready for more advanced drills which are designed to further the development of their game. Several such drills are presented in the following section.

19

LINE-OF-GOOD-POSITION AT THE NET

The basic principle of position play, "as your opponent makes his shot, be ready and waiting on the line-of-good-position, the line that bisects the angle of his possible returns,'' applies to net play as well as to baseline play. As is true in baseline play, a player at the net stands directly in the center of his court (on the center line) *only* when his opponent is hitting from the center of the baseline (Figure 25, A). When the opponent is hitting from near the sides of the court, the net man should be a step or two away from the center line, but in the same direction toward which his opponent has moved (Figure 25, B&C). The net man moves *toward* the ball (in contrast to moving *away* from the ball as a back courter would do), moving to the left if the deep man is moved to his right and moving to the right if the deep man is moved to his left; he is in the center of the court only when the deep man is also in the center (Figure 25, D).

20

CHANGING-GRIP VOLLEYING

Beginning players are usually taught to use their regular ground stroke grips for volleying. The theory is that since they are beginners they will be practicing and playing with other beginners. As beginners, all players will be hitting balls relatively easily. Volleyers, then, will have ample time to change grips from forehand to backhand and from backhand to forehand. Often, however, even beginners playing other soft-hitting beginners need specific practice in changing grips.

An effective drill for grip-changing practice is illustrated in Figure 26. A feeder feeds balls to a volleyer, with the feeder first standing about 12-15 feet behind the baseline (position 1 in Figure 26). He drops-and-feeds balls to the volleyer, mixing-up his feeds to give the net man both forehand and backhand volleys. Just prior to each feed, however, the feeder calls "Forehand!" or "Backhand!," telling the volleyer where the feed will be aimed. Because the feeder's ball will be in the air for a long time (he's feeding from well-behind the baseline), and because he tells the volleyer where he is planning to hit the ball (by calling "Forehand" or "Backhand"

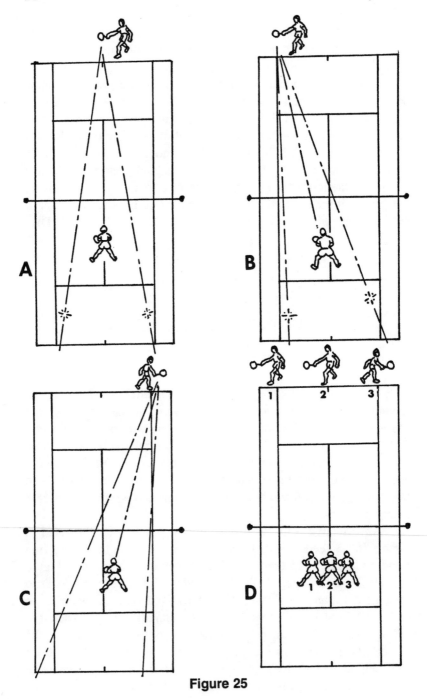

Figure 25

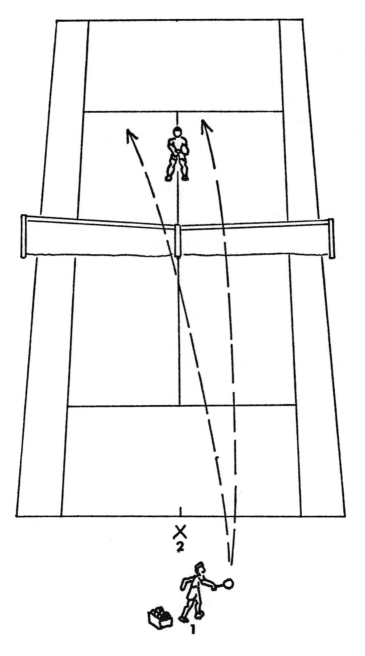

Figure 26

before he feeds), the volleyer is well-prepared to make the necessary grip change.

After the volleyer feels confident that he can change grips adequately, the feeder moves forward to about three to four feet behind the baseline (position 2, Figure 26). He then feeds from there, and drives the volley back at the net man if the ball is volleyed to him. The volleyer now has less time to change grips; he must change quickly.

21

MIXED VOLLEYS: FOREHANDS AND BACKHANDS

Having been given some practice in changing grips at the net, players are then ready to continue volleying forehands and backhands. A large group can be accommodated on one court in a drill called Mixed Volleys. For safety reasons, only two players should be permitted to volley at the same time on one court.

Volleyers take the normal volleying positions; feeders stand opposite each volleyer, across the net, standing just behind the service line. Feeders drop-and-hit balls, easily, directly to the volleyers, setting balls up for them. The volleyers attempt to hit the balls back easily. Other players act as retrievers around the court or wait their turns behind the volleyers. Volleyers volley for a few minutes, after which they move to the end of the waiting line as the next man in the waiting line moves into volleying position.

When all have acquired some skill, feeders are moved back to the baseline (Figure 27). They drop-and-hit to their volleyers. If the volley is made back to them, they drive the ball back at the volleyer, easily, trying to keep a rally going. When a rally is ended, the feeder drops another ball and another rally is started. Feeders are cautioned to stay on their half of the court, and volleyers are cautioned to hit straight ahead to their feeders.

Groups are rotated frequently so that all players get volleying practice.

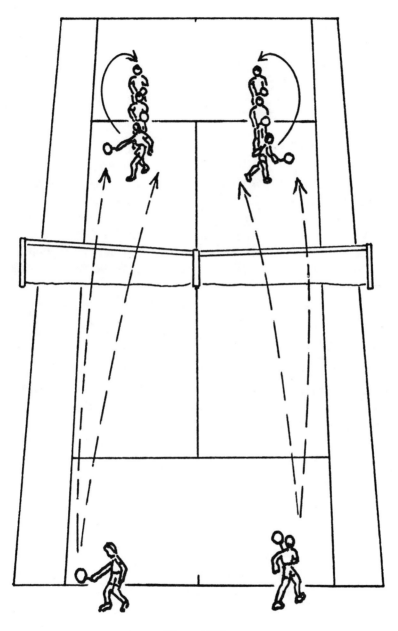

Figure 27

22

SCRAMBLE VOLLEYS

All players should be taught to scramble when they are volleying at the net, as well as when they are hitting ground strokes in the back court. Too often volleyers fail to even try to return a ball that is hit only a few feet away from them; they assume that they cannot reach the ball and don't even make an attempt to volley it. Many players, after some practice in a Scramble Volley drill (Figure 28), are surprised at how easily they can reach and volley attempted passing shots which, prior to practice in scramble volleying, they would not even have tried for.

The coach feeds balls to the volleyer by dropping-and-hitting, aiming balls to the left and right of the net man, in simulation of passing shots. Balls are fed in quick succession by the coach, who does not try to return the net man's volleys.

The volleyer is encouraged to "try for everything," to let no ball go past him without his trying to volley it. He soon learns to recover quickly after every shot and finds that he can move quickly to reach balls that previously were getting past him.

If a group of players is involved, players rotate from retrieving positions to waiting positions to volleying positions at regular intervals.

23

TWO-ON-ONE: VOLLEYS AND GROUND STROKES

In advanced play, a volleyer must be quick and agile; frequently he must volley while off balance or while in the midst of

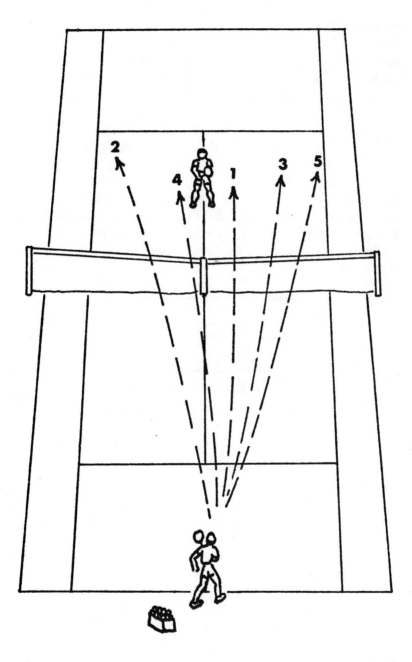

Figure 28

recovering from a previous shot. Moreover, he must be able to volley balls that are aimed sharply cross-court or down-the-line, for seldom in actual play does an advanced baseliner hit directly at a volleyer. A Two-on-One drill gives a volleyer practice in covering his court, in recovering quickly, and in volleying angled drives (Figure 29).

Two players play on a baseline, one on each side of the court. A volleyer starts in the center of the court in the normal volleying position. One of the back court players starts a rally by hitting to the volleyer, who volleys the ball to either corner. The ball is kept in play as the back courters, using hard-hit down-the-line shots, cross-court shots, and "dink" shots at the volleyer's feet, try to win the point. The volleyer tries to cut off all passing shots, digging out the low balls and slashing the high ones to the corners or angling them sharply.

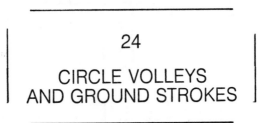

24

CIRCLE VOLLEYS AND GROUND STROKES

A group of players can be given practice in volleys and ground strokes on only one court.

Players form two files, one on each side of the net with one file in the backcourt and the other in the forecourt (Figure 30). The first player in either file starts a rally; the first player in the opposite file returns the ball (one player volleys, the other makes a ground stroke). Each player hits only once and, after he hits, moves quickly to the end of his file; the second player in each file moves forward to the hitting position, and these players try to sustain the rally, each moving to the end of his file after hitting only once. The ball is kept in play in this manner, with players rotating from the front to the rear of their files. When a miss occurs, a front player quickly starts another rally.

The drill can be restricted to forehands only, or to backhands only, or can be used for both forehands and backhands.

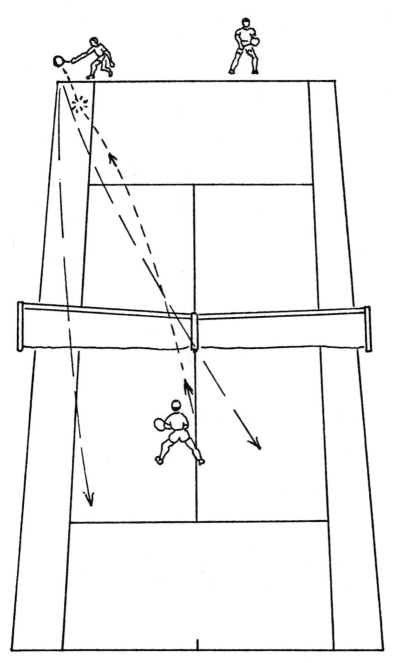

Figure 29

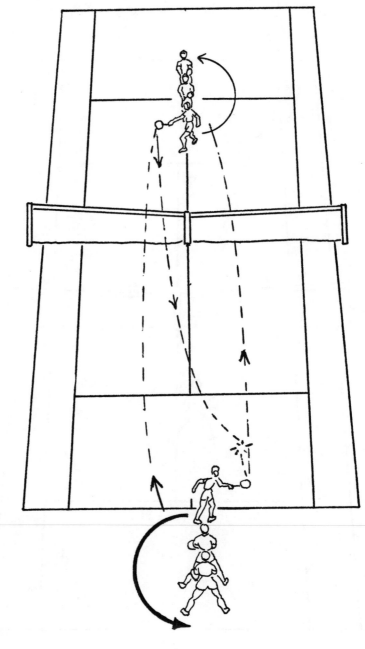

Figure 30

The drill can be made more difficult for intermediate players by restricting the area into which volleyers can hit to the back court, the area bounded by the baseline and the service line. It can be made even more difficult for advanced players through the addition of deep-lines drawn across the end of the court, about eight feet inside the baseline; volleys must then land inside the deep-area to be considered good.

Fun and friendly competition can be provided by the drill by having a contest: a point is scored against a player each time he misses. After a prescribed time period, the player with the fewest points is the winner.

If two units are working on one court (Double Circle Volleys and Ground Strokes, Figure 31), or if units on one court are competing against units on adjacent courts, each unit counts the number of consecutive hits it makes before a miss occurs. After a given time period, the unit that has the longest rally is the winner.

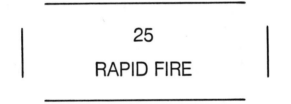

25

RAPID FIRE

Successful volleying in advanced play requires that a volleyer be extremely quick in moving to the ball, and in moving the racket. Through a drill called Rapid Fire, a player can quicken his reactions at the net (Figure 32).

A volleyer takes the normal volleying position. Three players take positions along the opposite baseline, each with eight or nine balls available. Player A drops-and-hits a ball at the volleyer. When this ball is about three-quarters of the way to the volleyer, Player B drops-and-hits a ball at the volleyer. When this ball is about three-quarters of the way to the net man, Player C drops-and-hits. Player A then hits another ball, then Player B, and so on.

The volleyer, meanwhile, tries to volley all balls hit to him. He must recover quickly after each shot, because another ball is already on its way toward him.

Players A, B, and C will quickly learn to time and stagger their

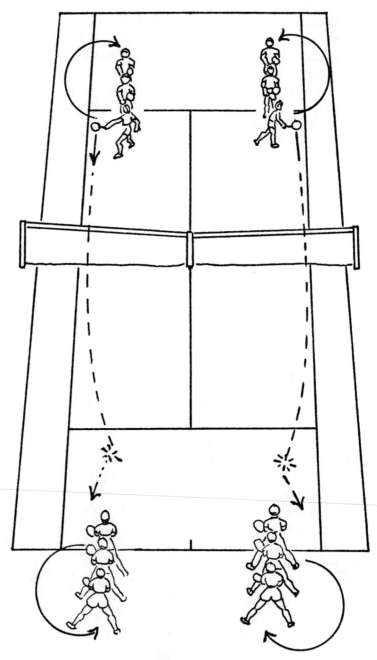

Figure 31

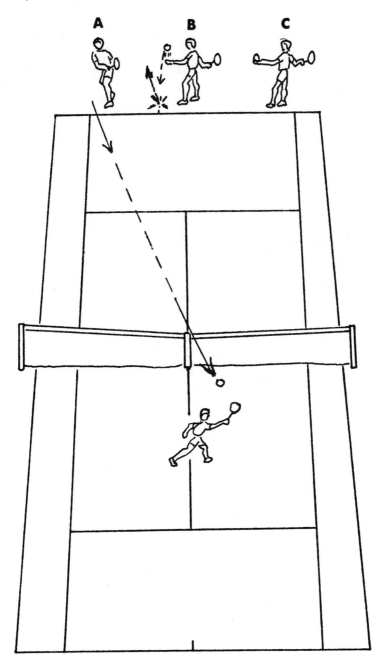

Figure 32

hits so that the volleyer will have to recover quickly after every shot and yet be in no danger of being hit by a ball. If A, B, and C all hit their shots at about the same speed the volleyer will be in no danger.

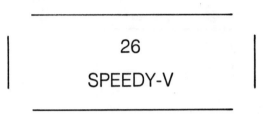

26

SPEEDY-V

One, two, or three units of two players each can improve their volleying skill, particularly their speed-of-reaction, by engaging in quick exchange volleys on one court (Figure 33). Two players (partners) stand opposite each other, each about eight feet from the net. One player starts a rally by feeding the ball to his partner. Both players then volley the ball, trying to keep it in play.

If only one unit is assigned to a court, the players volley astride the center line; if two units are assigned, each unit volleys on one side of the court, midway between the center line and a singles sideline; if three units are assigned, two volley astride the singles sidelines while the third volleys astride the center line.

Units can compete against each other, and against other units on adjacent courts: players are asked to volley as *often* as they can within a prescribed time period. A hit by either player counts as one. When a rally is ended, a new one is quickly started and the count continues (if the first rally ended at six, the new rally starts at seven). The unit with the greatest number of hits at the end of the time period is the winning one; players are thus encouraged to volley quickly and at good speed.

A variation to be used with less-experienced players is to have a marathon rally. Players are asked to rally as long as they can without missing. When a rally is ended, a new one is started with the count beginning at zero. Control, rather than speed, is thus emphasized. At the end of the time period, the unit that has the longest rally is the winning one.

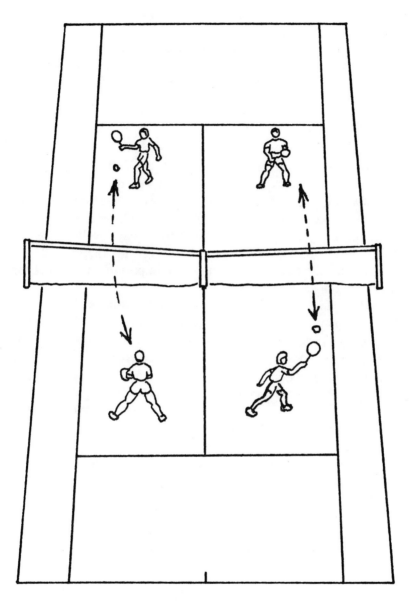

Figure 33

27

CIRCLE VOLLEYS

A group of players can be given practice in advanced volleying through use of a drill called Circle Volleys (Figure 34).

Players form two files, one on each side of the net, with the first man in each file in the normal volleying position. The first player in either file starts a rally with the first player in the opposite file, with each player volleying the ball. A player volleys the ball only once, then quickly moves to the end of his file. The second player in his file quickly moves to the front position, trying to keep the rally going.

He volleys the ball, then quickly moves to the end of his file; the next player moves up and volleys, and so on. Files rotate quickly, with each player volleying as the rotation brings him to the front position. When a ball is missed, another rally is started and rotation continues.

Two units can be in action on one court (Figure 35), one on each side of the court. Players must rotate, then, in the direction of the nearest side line to avoid bumping into other players. The units can compete against each other, and against other units on adjacent courts, in a contest to see which unit can keep the ball in play longest (the longest rally). Each unit keeps it's own count, counting out loud.

28

ANGLED VOLLEYS

A player can increase his quickness at the net and his ability to hit angled volleys by volleying to three other volleyers (Figure 36).

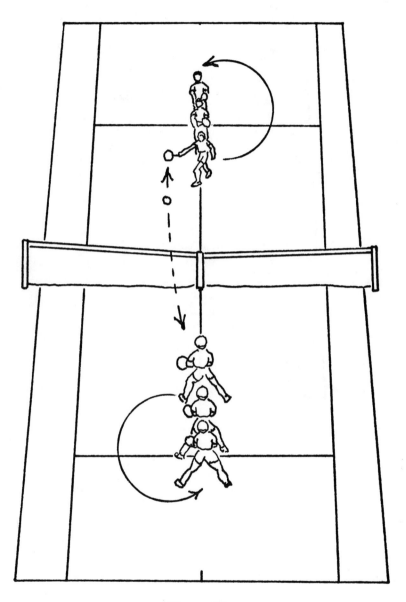

Figure 34

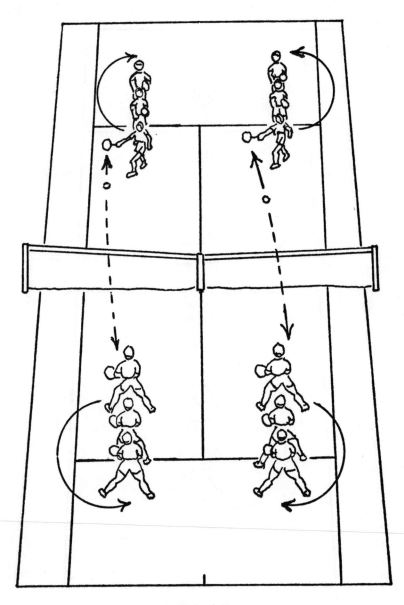

Figure 35

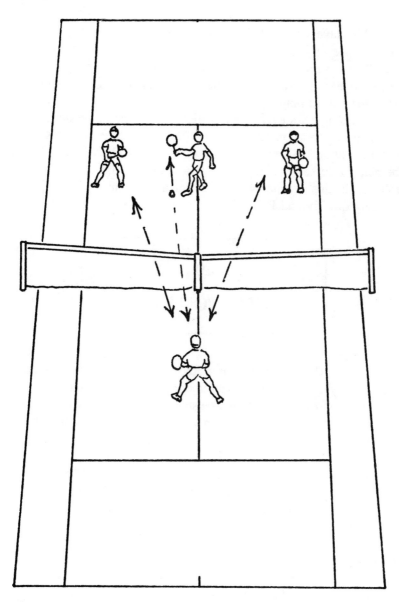

Figure 36

All players take positions about eight feet from the net. The single volleyer is in the center of the court, astride the center line; the other players spread out on their court, with one in the center and one each astride a singles sideline. All players then volley, trying to keep the ball in play.

The single volleyer tries to volley to the men on the sides of the court, trying to keep the ball away from the center man (his shots will be returned to him so quickly, however, that he will not always be able to do so). Regardless of where he hits the ball, however, rallying in this manner will give him a great deal of practice in reacting quickly and in handling angled volleys.

29

HALF VOLLEYS

The half volley is a shot that is seldom deliberately practiced, yet it is one that is an important part of a tennis player's arsenal of strokes. A player is usually forced to make the shot following a serve and an approach to the net. As he is usually forced to make it somewhere near the service line during the approach, the shot should be practiced in that position.

One, two, or three players can practice the shot by standing near the service line as a coach feeds balls. The coach feeds so that the balls land on or near the service line, directly at the feet of the volleyers (Figure 37).

A group of players can be accommodated on one court if they form files behind the half-volleyers, with the first player in each file making six or seven shots before he rotates to the end of his file as the second man in the file moves into the half-volleying position. A few group members can act as retrievers, keeping the coach supplied with balls.

All volleyers should remain near the service line as they practice the stroke. They should be reminded, however, that in actual play they would move forward to the ideal volleying position after making a half volley.

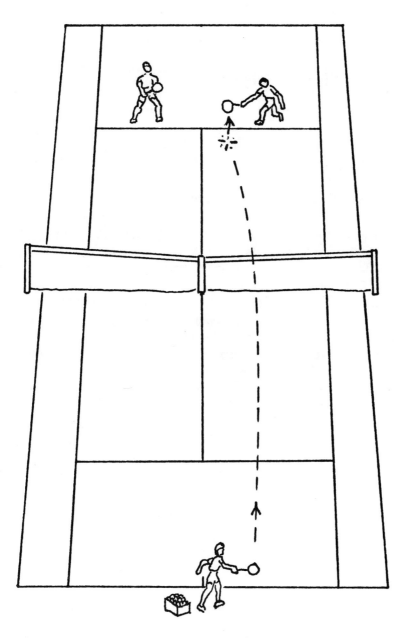

Figure 37

30

DRIVE VOLLEYS

The drive volley, like the half volley, is an important part of a player's repertoire of strokes, and it, too, is seldom practiced.

A drill very similar to that used in practicing the half volley is an effective one for giving players practice in this stroke. Hitters play just behind the service line as a coach feeds slow, lazy floaters to them from deep in the opposite court (Figure 38). Hitters are encouraged to use a short swing drive to play the balls.

Both forehand and backhand shots can be practiced, depending upon the placement of the coach's feed. Hitters should at first start in the mid-court position and practice the shot. When they have acquired some feel for the stroke, they should start on the baseline and run forward to drive volley the coach's feed and then continue on to the ideal volleying position.

As in other drills, several players can be accommodated on one court by having players form files and rotate from hitting position to waiting position to retrieving position. For safety reasons, not more than two players should be in the hitting position at any one time.

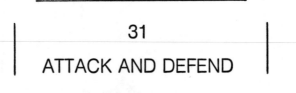

31

ATTACK AND DEFEND

A drill called Attack and Defend (Figure 39), in which five players are engaged at one time, gives players practice in mid-court defensive shots and in forecourt attacking shots.

Three players spread out along a service line (the defending team), two players play in the normal volleying positions (the at-

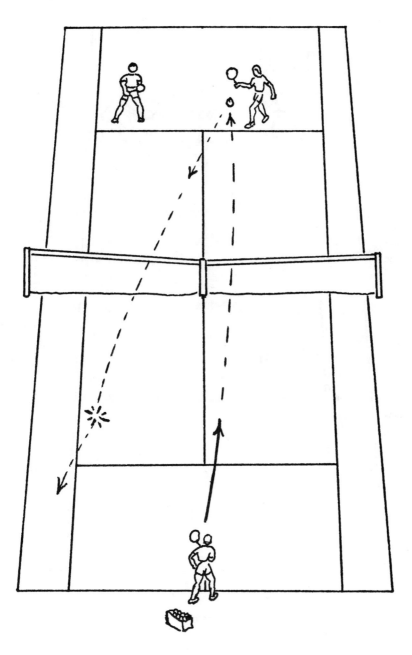

Figure 38

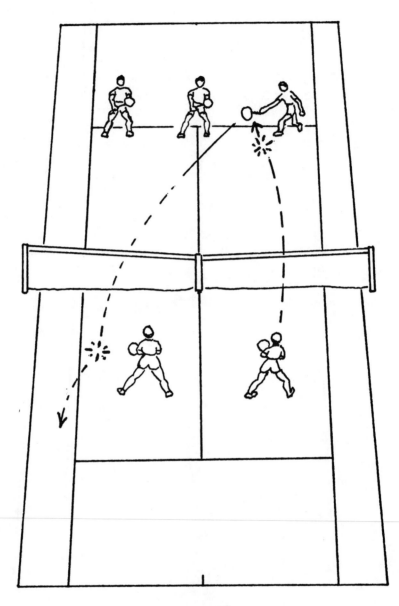

Figure 39

tacking team). Any player starts a rally. The attackers, if they get a fairly high ball, try to slash the ball away for a winner, aiming at the feet of one of the defenders. The defenders try to play balls low to the attackers feet, trying to make them hit up so that they cannot attack. If the attackers are forced to hit up, the defenders should anticipate a weak return and should be ready to move in on the ball to play it high, if possible, and become the attackers.

Players rotate regularly so all get practice in the attacking position and in the defending position.

IV

Lob Drills

The lob is one of the least spectacular strokes in tennis, yet it is one of the most important, particularly at low levels of play where players seldom have strong overhead smashes. Because a lobbed ball must clear a net man and still land inside the baseline, the stroke requires a good deal of touch and feel; this touch and feel can best be acquired through specific drills that give a player practice in the stroke.

32
LOBBING A DROPPED BALL

For a beginner, initial practice in the lob should consist of hitting a self-dropped ball. Standing about three or four feet behind the baseline, he should drop the ball, let it bounce, then hit it upward and forward, over the net, so that it clears an imaginary opponent standing at the net in the opposite court and lands inside the baseline. Both forehands and backhands should be practiced.

When he has acquired some touch for the shot and can hit most dropped balls so that they land inside the baseline, he should force himself to run a short distance—as if he were running in actual play to reach a ball—and then lob. His toss now should be upward and away from him so that it bounces six to eight feet from him. He should then run to the ball and lob it after it bounces. Again, he should practice both forehands and backhands. He should also vary the direction of the toss, tossing some balls so that he must move obliquely forward, some so that he must move obliquely backward, and others so that he must move sideward.

33

LOBBING A TOSSED BALL

When a beginner has acquired some feel and touch for the lob by lobbing a dropped ball, he should begin lobbing a tossed ball.

A practice partner (or coach), standing at the net, should toss balls to the lobber, who is standing about three feet behind the baseline. The balls should be tossed so that they bounce a few feet in front of the lobber, who plays the ball on the first bounce and lobs it over the head of the tosser.

When the lobber acquires some proficiency in lobbing these easy tosses, the balls should be tossed away from him so that he must run to play them. He should be given practice in running in various directions—forward, backward, and to the side—and various distances.

34

LOBBING A DRIVEN BALL

Having had some practice in lobbing tossed balls, a player is then ready to begin practice in lobbing driven balls. He'll need a practice partner, who agrees to feed him drives, so that he can practice his lob.

Both players play in the backcourt, about two feet behind their baselines. The feeder drops-and-hits, driving the ball over the net to the lobber, who lobs the ball back. The ball should be fed to both forehand and backhand sides of the lobber, and should be directed a few feet away from him so that he must run to reach it.

Following this drill, both players should rally, each driving the ball over the net. The player who needs lobbing practice should lob every third or fourth ball that is driven by his partner.

And finally, the lobber's partner can pounce on any short drive, hit the ball deep to the corner of the opposite court, and advance to the net. The lobber then can practice lobbing over the net man.

V

Overhead Smash Drills

The overhead smash, like the serve, is one of the power strokes of tennis. As the answer to the lob, it is usually a hard-hit, spectacular shot, but one that demands delicate judgment and timing and requires a good deal of practice.

Beginners can be given excellent practice in learning the rudiments of the stroke through the use of the drills presented in the section on Group Teaching (Chapter 9), modifying the group drills to suit their needs. Additional drills, more advanced than those in the section on Group Instruction, are presented in the following section.

35

ANGLE SMASHING

A smasher can most efficiently be given practice in placing his smashes to the corners of the court if three players act as retrievers and lobbers, returning his smashes (Figure 40). Spread out deep, these three players can reach most of the smashes, lobbing

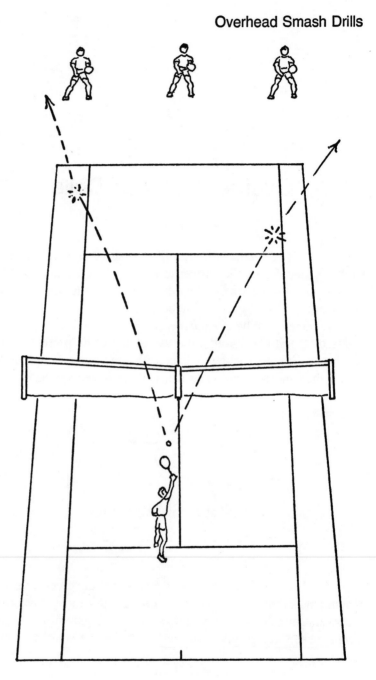

Figure 40

them back, so that very little time is wasted in chasing and picking up balls.

The smash is an enervating stroke. A smasher tires quickly because of the strenuous motion required to smash, so players should be rotated frequently.

A doubles team can also be given practice in smashing and in developing team work by having a team smash to three lobbers (Figure 41).

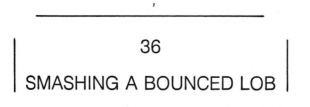

36

SMASHING A BOUNCED LOB

A very high lob is a difficult one to smash. The ball is usually descending almost straight down with a lot of speed, and thus is difficult to time precisely. Most good players let these very high lobs bounce and then smash them. Surprisingly to some players, these shots are not as easy as they would appear; thus they require specific practice.

Two baseliners can lob to the smasher, lobbing high so that the ball descends almost vertically (Figure 42). The smasher lets each lobbed ball bounce, then smashes it back to the lobbers. Smashers will find that when they smash from close to the net, they can hit the ball relatively flat, and that when they smash from deep in the court, they will have to spin the ball a bit in order to make it bend and hook downward after it crosses the net.

Figure 41

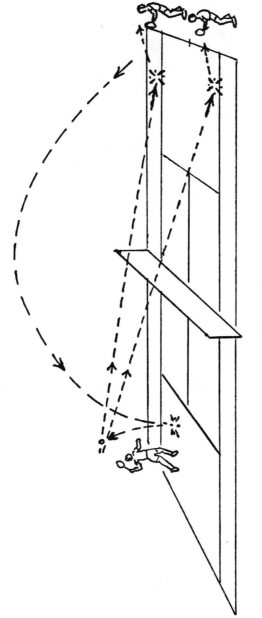

Figure 42

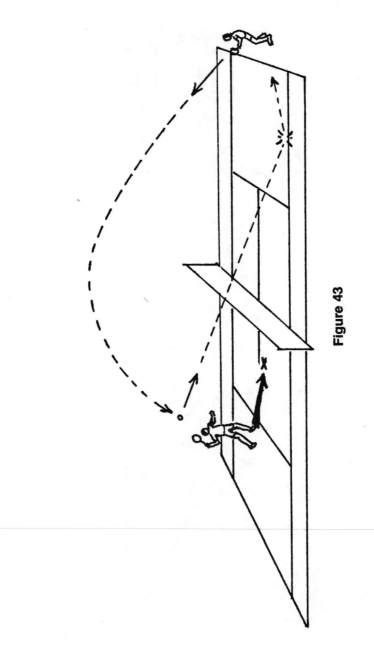

Figure 43

37

SMASH AND RECOVER

Smashers should learn to recover quickly after smashing so that they can deal with the next shot should it be a drive or a passing shot.

One player, standing in the backcourt, feeds a mixture of lobs and drives to a hitter playing in the volleying position in the opposite court (Figure 43). The backcourt man tries to dislodge the net man by forcing him back with a lob; he then tries to hit to his feet or to pass him. The smasher recovers quickly after every smash, moving forward and sideward to be on the line-of-good-position for the next shot. The ball is kept in play in this manner, with the deep man lobbing, forcing the net man back, then driving the smash back at the net man.

VI

Miscellaneous Stroke Drills

Beginning and low-intermediate tennis should be, and usually is, back court tennis. Because neither player can volley effectively, both should play in the back court and advance to the net only when they are forced to in order to reach a short ball. Even at this level of play, however, players should be aware of basic tactical principles which, if followed, make for more successful play.

38

HIT CROSS COURT FOR DEFENSE

All players should be aware of the importance of returning a hard, aggressive shot cross-court. Cross-court shots keep a player in the rally by minimizing the distance he has to run to retrieve a ball. In Figure 44, if player H were to hit his backhand down-the-line so that his opponent can play his shot from position N, player H would conceivably have to scramble wide to the right to reach a ball aimed at the opening on his forehand side (along line D3). If player H were to hit his backhand cross-court to his

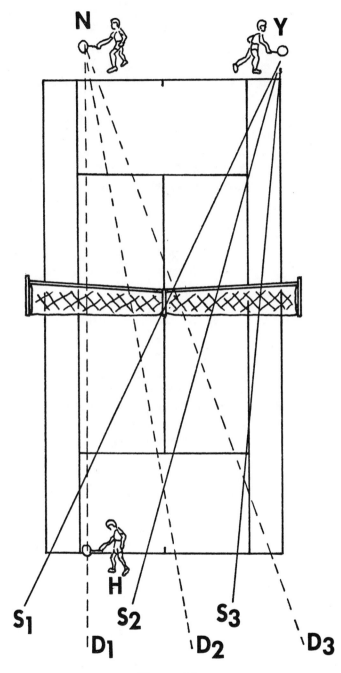

Figure 44

opponent's backhand, however, he would have to scramble no farther than line S3 to retrieve a ball aimed at the opening on his forehand side.

By hitting cross-court, too, player H has brought his line-of-good-position (S2) closer to his hitting position; if he were to hit down-the-line, his line-of-good-position would be D2, some 2 or 3 steps farther from his hitting position.

This same tactic should be employed in the forehand corner. Balls should be hit cross-court to minimize the distance to the far side and to bring the line-of-good-position closer to the hitter (Figure 45).

39

RETURNING THE SERVE

Beginners, because they are usually playing other beginners, seldom are faced with the problem of returning hard serves; most often the serves they must return are slow or medium-paced ones. Unless they have unusually strong ground strokes—what beginner has?—they should be content merely to return even these easy serves in a safe and cautious way, avoiding risky returns.

The safest return usually is one that forces the server to go backward to play a backhand, because almost all beginners are extremely weak on deep backhands. The ball need not be aimed close to the sideline or to the baseline—such a shot is too risky for a beginner—but reasonably deep and sufficiently to the side of the court to keep the server from running around his backhand.

Hitting to the server's backhand, when the serve is made from the right court, violates the cardinal rule of "hit cross-court for defense." It compels the receiver to move a longer distance to be on his line-of-good-position than would a cross-court return, but because the server usually has a weaker backhand than a forehand, this violation is not likely to be of serious consequence. If the server has a strong backhand, however, the best return is cross-court, to his

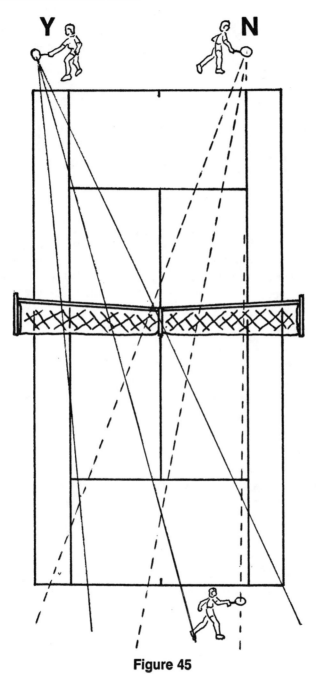

Figure 45

forehand. If the receiver has a very strong forehand, too, he can aim his return sharply cross-court, but in general, his safest play is to make the server go backward to play a deep backhand (Figures 46, 47).

40

KILLER-SERVE RETURN

A coach often has difficulty in providing his players with practice in returning hard, fast serves, particularly when the hardest server on his squad has only what the coach would assess as a medium-speed serve. The speed of anyone's serve can be increased, from the receiver's point of view, if the serve is made from well inside the baseline. A serve made from this position reaches the receiver in less time than one made from the normal serving position; moreover, it comes to the receiver from a higher point (at a greater angle) than one made from deeper in the court. A short player's serve, one that comes in low and relatively easy when served from the regular serving position, is thus converted to a tall player's serve, one that comes in higher and harder, when served from inside the baseline. The short player can thus be used to provide serves similar to those produced by a tall player.

The squad is divided into servers and receivers. Receivers play in the normal receiving position, but servers serve from about six feet inside the baseline (this distance can vary, depending upon the speed of serve desired). Servers serve as hard as they can; receivers try to return the serves (Figure 48).

Two, three, or four players can be assigned to each unit. They rotate regularly so that all get practice in returning hard serves.

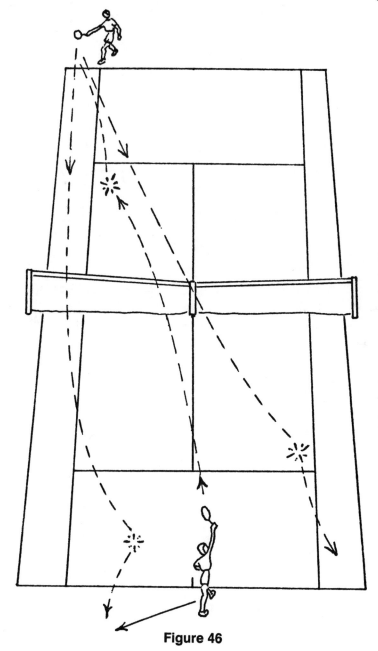

Figure 46

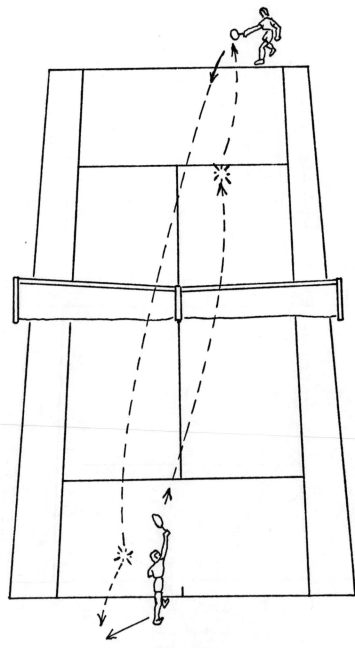

Figure 47

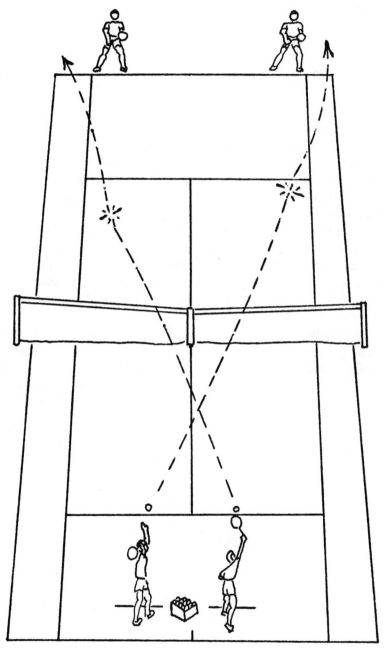

Figure 48

41

SUICIDE!

Quite frequently a doubles player is caught in mid-court as one of his opponents smashes the ball at him. Usually, a player in this position makes only a half-hearted attempt to return the smash; frequently he makes no attempt what-so-ever, merely turning his back on the ball to avoid being hit by it. Yet, it is surprising how often such smashes will be returned if a player learns not to give up on the shot, but to try to get the ball back. A drill called Suicide!, in which a smasher deliberately hits to the feet of a man in mid-court gives a player practice in returning these difficult smashes, and often convinces him that if he tries to get the ball back he will occasionally be successful (Figure 49).

One player lobs from deep in one corner of the court feeding medium-high, medium-deep lobs to a smasher while his partner stands in mid-court. The smasher aims at the mid-court man's feet. The mid-court man tries to get the ball back any way he can; he'll get very few balls back, but, in actual play, getting one such ball back could mean the difference between winning and losing a match.

42

THE AUSSIE SPECIAL

A drill that is used by the Australian Davis Cup team is an excellent one for conditioning and for developing quickness and defensive ability.

Using chalk, tape, or tempera paint, mark the court so that it is divided down the middle, as shown in Figure 50. One player (A,

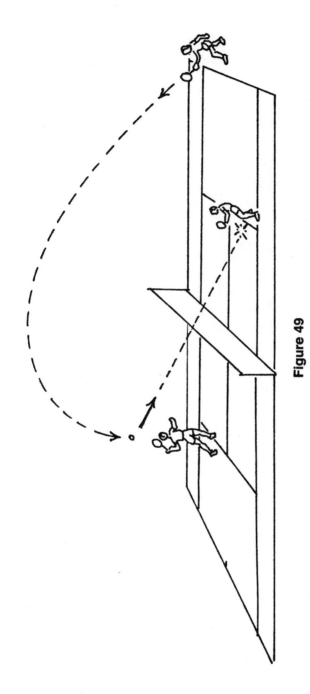

Figure 49

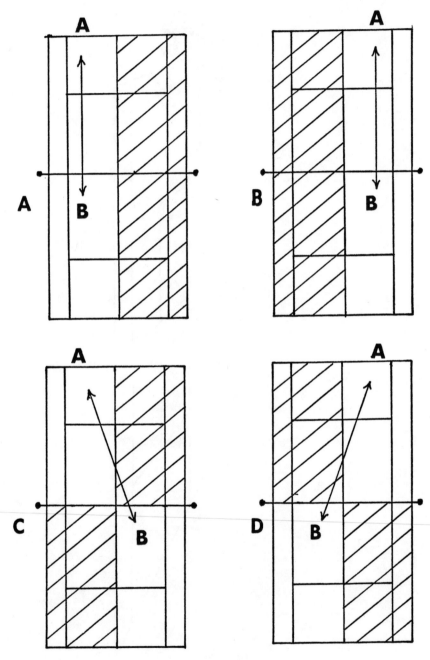

Figure 50

Figure 50), covers the forehand back court, including the alley. His practice opponent, B, plays at the net on the backhand side. Each player holds several balls, with several more balls being placed at the net where player B can quickly pick them up. A rally is started and each player tries to pass the other or to make a placement. As soon as a rally ends, another one is quickly started by either player. Each player tries to get to every ball to maintain the rally.

Variations:

Figure 50, B: Player A plays deep in the backhand court, B plays at the net on the forehand side.

Figure 50, C: Player A plays deep in the forehand court, B plays net on the forehand side.

Figure 50, D: Player A plays deep in the backhand court, B plays net on the backhand side.

The drills can be expanded by having player A hit against two players, B and C, with A first in the right forecourt, then the left forecourt, while B and C are in the backcourt (Figure 51). Then, A moves to the backcourt, first to the right then to the left, and B and C play at the net.

43

THE DROP SHOT

The drop shot can be learned in successive stages, with the learner "sneaking up" on the complete stroke (Figure 52).

Stage 1. A feeder, on the baseline, drops-and-hits to the hitter who is standing on the opposite baseline, deliberately hitting short so that the hitter can play the ball well inside his baseline on the first bounce. The hitter drop-shots the ball, swinging forward and downward to impart backspin to it. In the early stages of learning the stroke, he should be content merely to make the ball land about mid-way between the service line and the net.

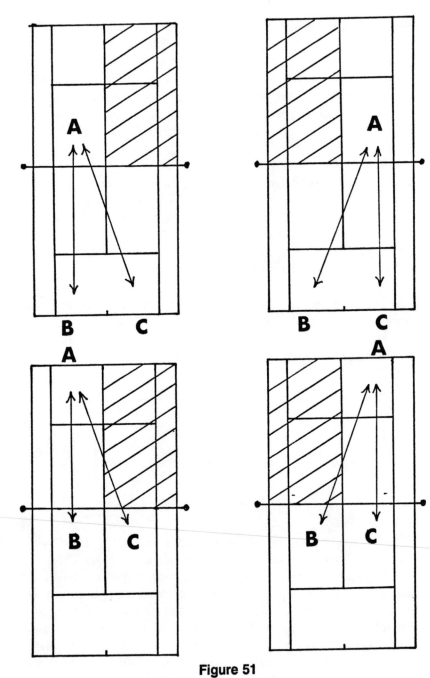

Figure 51

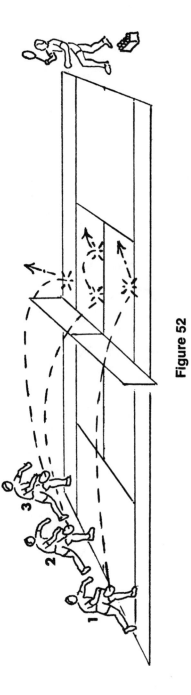

Figure 52

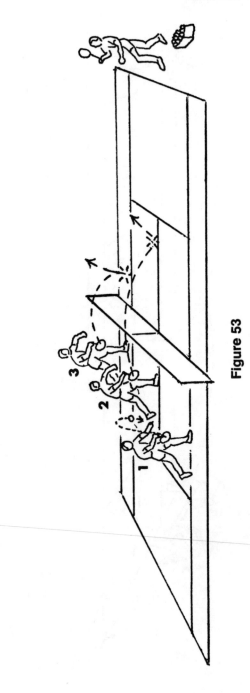

Figure 53

Stage 2. When he has acquired some feel for the stroke, he should add more backspin to the ball and change the trajectory of his shots so that the ball falls more vertically after it crosses the net; his objective now is to make the ball bounce twice before it reaches the service line.

Stage 3. Finally, he imparts still more spin to the ball and tries to drop it barely over the net so that it falls almost vertically, bounces very close to the net, and rises almost vertically after the bounce. It is helpful if the hitter pretends he is trying to hit the ball into a basket that is placed about six feet from the net.

44

THE DROP VOLLEY

The drop volley, like the drop shot, is a shot that requires good timing and touch. The key concept in making the shot is that of cushioning the impact of the ball on the racket. The racket face, instead of being jabbed at the ball as it is in a normal volley, is deadened or drawn backward a bit just as it meets the ball. This deadening of the racket face is combined with a slight "cupping" action—the top edge of the racket face is turned back a bit just as the ball is struck—to impart a little backspin to the ball; the ball then "plops" up off the racket face and falls very short in the court. The backspin on it keeps it from bouncing forward, thus making the shot a difficult one for a baseliner to retrieve.

Like the drop shot, the drop volley can be learned in stages (Figure 53). A feeder on the baseline drives the ball to a hitter at the net. The hitter, playing the ball before it bounces, merely bunts the ball to himself, bunting it upward so that he can catch it on the fly with his non-hitting hand (stage 1).

The next step is that of bunting the ball a little harder so that it clears the net and lands inside the service line in the opposite court (stage 2). The final step is that of bunting the ball so that it clears the net and lands very close to it (stage 3).

VII

Doubles Drills

Beginning and low-intermediate players should play a kind of doubles different from that played by advanced players. Lacking strong serves, quick volleying ability, and decisive overhead smashes, most of their play should be confined to a one-up-one-back style. Playing side by side, each player on a team is usually responsible for covering, approximately, one side of the court—an area bounded by a doubles sideline and an imaginary line drawn down the center of the court.

45

BASIC POSITIONS

The Serving Team

When serving from the right court (Figure 54), the server should stand five or six feet to the right of the center mark. This will put him in good position to return any balls hit wide to his alley. His serves, from this position, can be placed to the receiver's backhand or be hit wide to the receiver's forehand. The wide serve is usually effective at this level of play, because it forces the re-

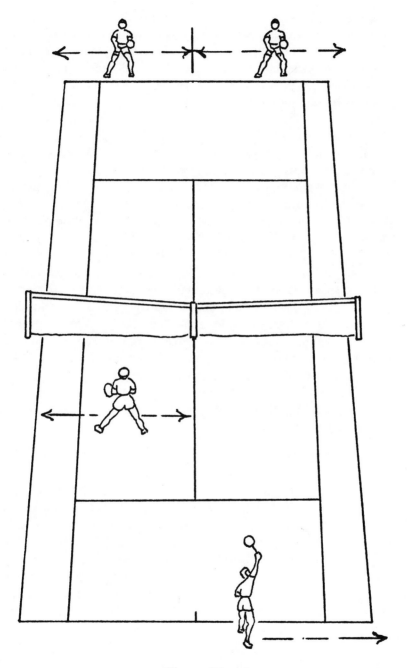

Figure 54

ceiver to make a very good cross-court shot in order to keep the ball away from the server's partner (who is playing at the net).

When serving from the left court (Figure 55), the server should stand two or three feet to the left of the middle of his side of the court. From this position he can serve wide to the receiver's backhand, again forcing the receiver to make a good cross-court shot to keep the ball away from the net man. The server, too, is in good position after the serve to return any balls hit wide to his alley, and is able, often, to run around balls hit slightly to his backhand side to play them with his stronger forehand stroke.

The server's partner, despite lacking volleying ability, should play in the forecourt, five or six feet from the net and about four or five feet inside the singles sideline. This position is slightly closer to the net than that used in more advanced doubles play, but a beginning player will find it easier to volley from this close-to-the-net position. His main responsibility, in this position, is to protect his alley; he should let no balls go past him down the alley. He should also protect against attempts at lobbing over his head, returning those lobs he can reach while letting the server return the deeper ones. The server, of course, will have to cross over to the net man's side of the court to do so; the net man simultaneously crosses to the server's side of the court to protect that side.

The net man should also cover shots made toward the center of the court, but only those which he can reach without taking more than a step or two toward the center line.

The Receiving Team

The receiving team, in beginner's doubles, should use the both-back position, with both the receiver and his partner playing on the baseline. Each player, then, is responsible for covering one side of the court. Balls hit down the middle of the court, between the two players, should be returned by the player who is in the left court, as he can play these balls with his strong forehand. Both players stay back to play balls that land deep in their court. Most of their returns should be directed away from the opposing net man, deep to the opposing back court man.

If either player on the receiving team is forced to run well forward to play a short ball, he should hurry to the ball, get it waist high if possible, and hit it deep to the opposing back court man. His

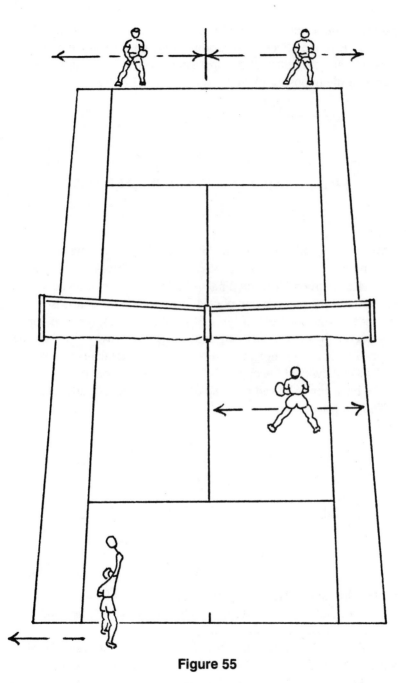

Figure 55

partner should run forward with him so that both players are in the forecourt, in the attacking position. They are then in ideal position to slash the next return at the opposing net-man or through the hole between the opposing players.

46

HIT IN FRONT OF YOUR PARTNER

Quite often doubles players, whether they be beginners, intermediates, or advanced players, find themselves in the one-up, one-back position. The cardinal principle to be employed in this situation, if the ball is being played from deep in the court, is to "hit in front of your partner" (Figure 56). Such a shot forces the opposing player to make a difficult shot cross-court away from the net man. If this return is not accurately placed, the net man can cut if off and slash it away at the opposing net man, or, if both opponents are in the back court, he can hit deep down the middle or angle the ball sharply for a winner.

47

NET MAN PROTECTS HIS ALLEY

The primary responsibility of a man at the net is to protect his alley. He should be eager to cut off any cross-court returns or slow floaters he can reach, but above all, he should let nothing go past him down the alley.

To cover his alley, he should move slightly toward the alley when an opponent is forced to hit from wide in the court (Figure 57). How far he should move depends upon how the opponent must

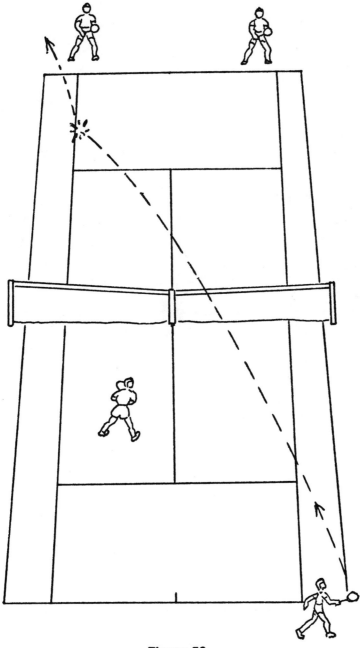

Figure 56

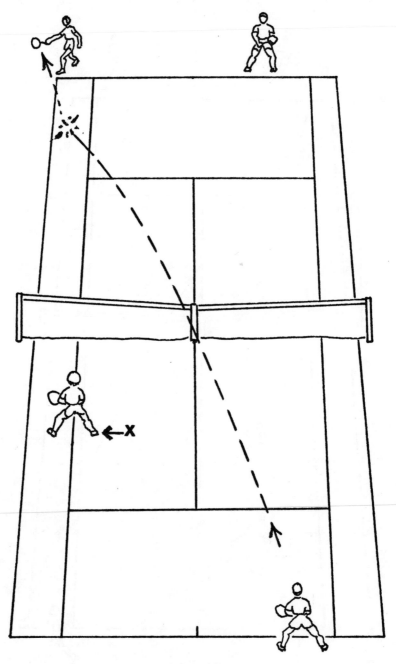

Figure 57

move. If the opponent is forced very wide, well beyond the alley, the net man should move well to the side of his normal net position. While protecting his alley, he should be ready, also, to take advantage of any poorly hit, cross-court shot by the opponent, stepping toward the ball if he can reach it with a step or two and volleying it either at the opposing net man's feet or through the opening between the opposing players.

48

HITTER DECIDES WHEN TO GO UP

When playing in the backcourt, doubles players frequently get confused about going to the net when the opponents give them a short ball to hit. Quite often, one player goes up, assuming his partner will go up also, and suddenly finds himself at the net alone, his partner having decided not to go up. Clearly this is not a desirable position to be in, as it creates a wide opening between the one-up one-back players.

This confusion can be avoided if both players understand that the hitter decides whether to go up or to stay back. He knows better than the other player how difficult his shot is. If he feels that he can make a forceful return of it, he will decide to follow the return to the net. If he anticipates that his return will cause little or no difficulty for the opponents, he will decide to stay back. In either case, his partner should watch him and react according to what the hitter decides to do (Figure 58).

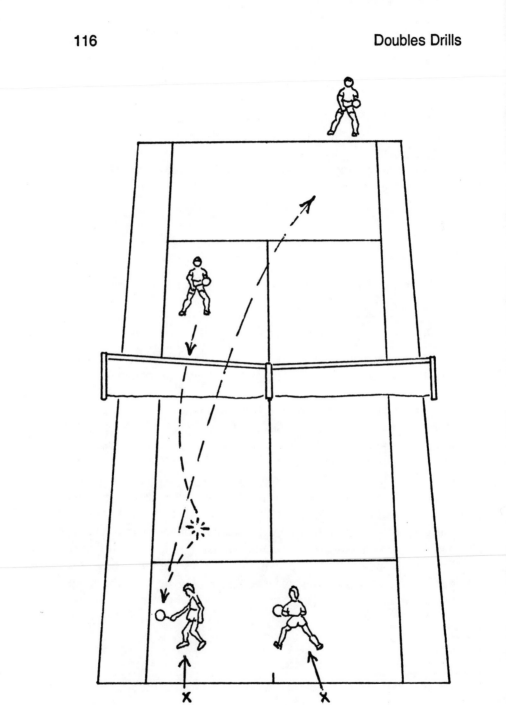

Figure 58

49

CLOSE THE OPENINGS

Doubles players should be aware of the necessity of covering up for their partners. If one player is forced wide to play a ball, the opening between him and his partner is increased. His partner, realizing this, should move toward the ball to close the opening. If, as in Figure 59 for example, Player A is forced to move to his right to play a ball, his partner (Player B) should move to the right also to close the gap down the middle. As Player B moves to the right, he creates a small opening on his left, but this is of much less consequence than is leaving the bigger opening down the middle.

Player D on the opposing team should also close the opening that exists on his left (down the alley) as Player A plays a shot from wide in the court. Player D should move a step or two toward the sideline, thus closing the opening here.

50

HIGH-INTERMEDIATE AND ADVANCED DOUBLES

Higher level doubles differs from beginner's play in that all four players attempt to play at the net. The net position is the attacking one, and players try to get to this position as quickly as possible (Figures 60, 61).

The server's partner plays at the net, eight or nine feet from it and about four feet from the doubles side line. The server, after serving, rushes forward to join his partner at the net. Each player,

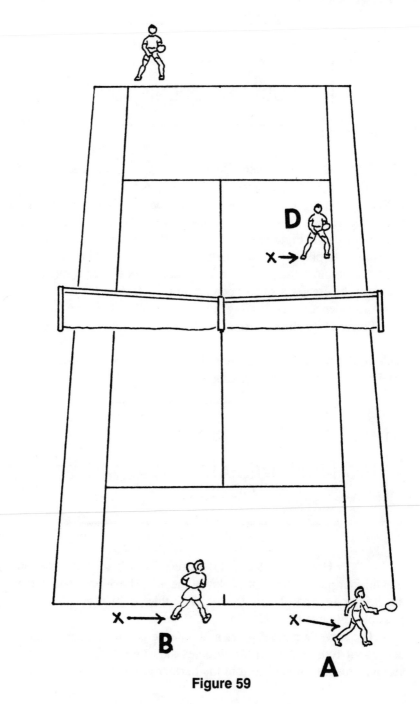

Figure 59

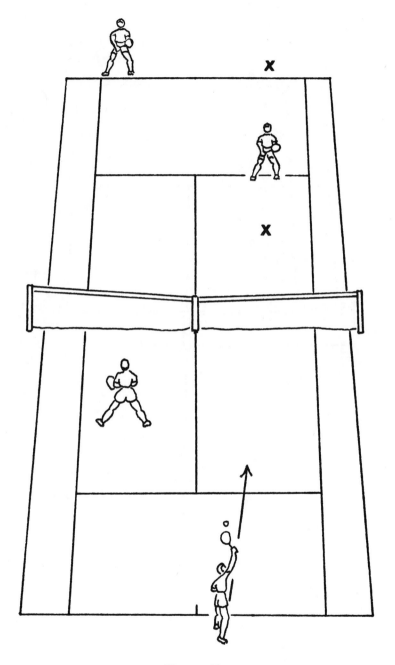

Figure 60

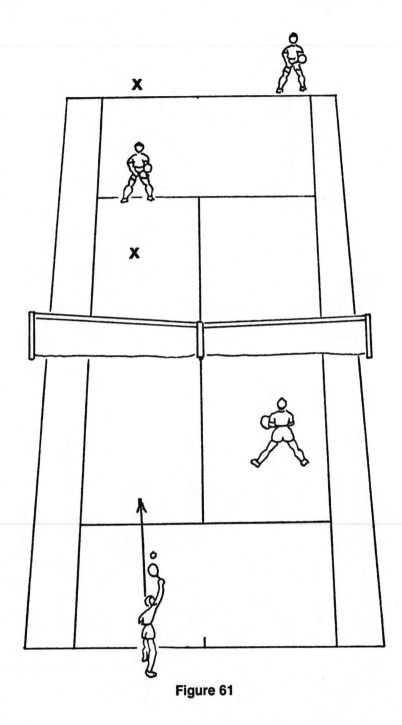

Figure 61

then, covers one side of the court while playing in the forecourt area.

The receiver of the serve, if he can handle the serve fairly well, tries to return the serve to the feet of the server, who is advancing to the net. Occasionally, the serve is returned by being lobbed over the net man's head.

The receiver's partner plays either on the service line, or close to the net, or on the baseline, depending upon how well his partner can return the serve. If the serve can be returned fairly easily, the receiver's partner plays on the service line or forward of it, so that he can deal with an anticipated weak return. If the serve is difficult to handle, he plays on the baseline so as not to be vulnerable to an easy shot given to the opponents by a weak service return. Regardless of where the receiver's partner plays, both he and the receiver try to get to the net as quickly as possible, looking and waiting for a short ball which they can pounce on, hit aggressively or low to the opponent's feet, and follow to the net.

Seldom are rallies long and drawn-out in high-level doubles. Most often, they consist only of a serve, the return of serve, and two or three volleys. Frequently lobs and overhead smashes are used, but in general, volleys, half-volleys, and low drives are used, with all four players trying to advance to the net.

51

SERVE AND GO UP: DOUBLES

Players should be given practice in approaching the net behind the serve as they would in doubles (Figure 62). Two players on the receiving team take normal doubles receiving positions (one-up, one-back). One player on the serving team assumes the server's partner position at the net. The coach serves, the player standing next to him advances to the net, and the point is played. All players then rotate: those at the net join the ends of their files, the receiver and the net-rusher stay at the net, and other players move

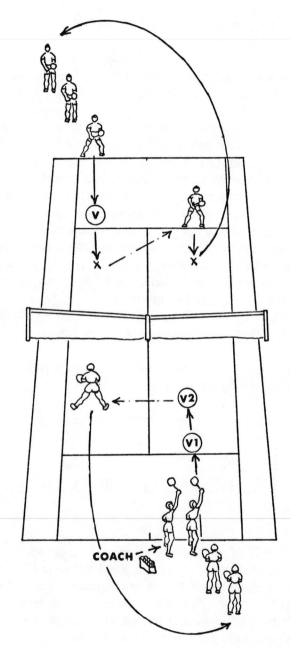

Figure 62

forward in their files. Another point is then played as the coach serves again. Players continue to rotate after every point. Groups are rotated, too, so that all players get practice in both advancing to the net and in returning the serve.

52

ARIZONA SPECIAL: DOUBLES

After having learned the proper approach to the net behind the coach's serve, players are ready to make the serve themselves and advance to the net (Figure 63).

Players form two files, one in a serving position and one in a receiving position (right or left courts), with a server's partner and a receiver's partner at the net. The first player in the serving file serves and advances to the net, the first player in the receiving file returns the serve and then advances to the net, also. The point is played to its completion, after which the players rotate: the server and receiver stay at the net, the players who were at the net go to the end of their files, and the next players in the file serve and receive. Rotation continues after every point. Play is alternated between right court and left court at regular intervals.

53

RETURN SERVE TO SERVER'S FEET

As the server advances to the net following his serve, he is, for a brief instant, in the mid-court area commonly referred to as "the danger-zone" or "no man's land." The receiver of the

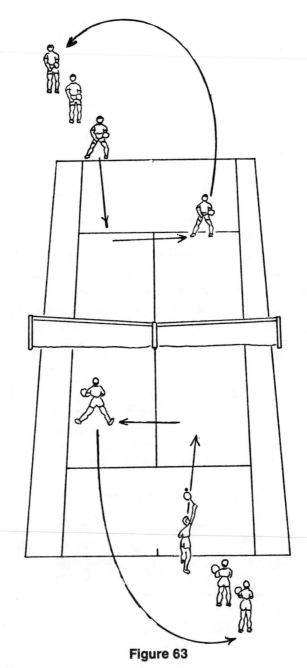

Figure 63

serve should try to exploit this weakness in position by aiming his
return at the server's feet, trying to force the server to hit up, to
make a low volley or a half-volley (Figure 64). Because he has to hit
up, the server will not be able to hit hard. Unless he places the ball
carefully away from the receiver's partner who is at the net, both he
and his partner are vulnerable to a shot made by the net man.

The return of serve need not be a hard hit shot. A hard hit shot
is much less desirable than a low shot to the server's feet, though the
ideal shot is a fast, low one, as it will force the net-rusher to volley
or half-volley from deep in the court. The deeper the net-rusher is
when he returns the shot, the more time the net man has to intercept
his return and the more time the receiver of the serve has to advance
to the net behind his return-of-serve. In any case, however, the
return-of-serve should generally be made directly back at the advancing server's feet.

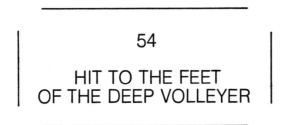

54

HIT TO THE FEET
OF THE DEEP VOLLEYER

When both players of a double team are at the net, their
positions are usually staggered somewhat; one player will be
slightly closer to the net than the other. Usually, the player closest to
the ball—the one in front of the ball—is slightly closer than the
other one.

An opposing team should take advantage of this staggered
position by aiming most of their shots to the feet of the deep man.
Because the man is deep, it is easy to hit low balls to him, forcing
him to hit up. His return is likely to be hit easy, then, giving the
opposing net man a good opportunity to intercept it and to slash it
away for a winner (Figure 65).

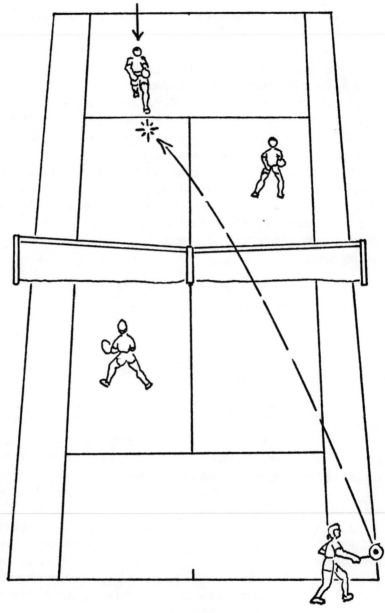

Figure 64

Figure 65

55

SET YOUR PARTNER UP
FOR THE KILL

. Doubles is a team game. Players should adopt a frame of mind that makes them want to make their partner look good. Each player tries to set his partner up for the kill.

The best way for a player to do this is to avoid trying to win a point by going for the "big" shot unless he is absolutely certain he can make a "big" shot. If any uncertainty exists in his mind, he is much better off merely trying to force the opponents to make a weak shot which his partner can put away for a winner. Usually, low shots to the feet of the opposing players will result in this weak shot. At worse, such a low shot will avoid putting his partner on the spot (Figure 66).

The best doubles player is not always the hard, spectacular hitter. Most often he is an easy, cagey hitter who deftly maneuvers his opponents out of position, or forces them to make difficult shots, so that his partner can easily finish off a rally. He sets his partner up so that he can make the winning shot.

56

NET MAN KEYS
ON THE OPPONENTS

When all four players in a doubles match are at the net engaged in an exchange, the ball travels only a short distance between hits so play is usually fast and quick. It is imperative that a

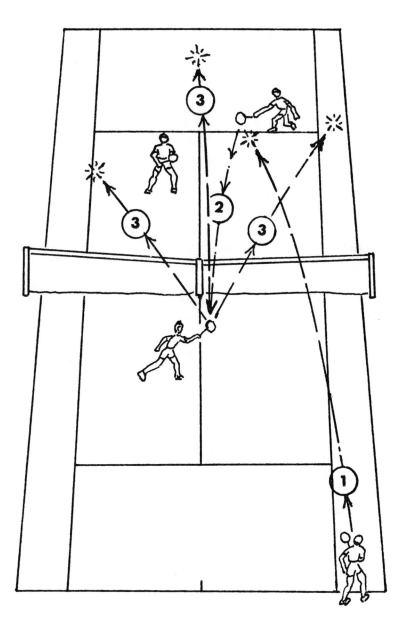

Figure 66

player in such an exchange see the ball early and well so that he can react quickly.

He will react most quickly if he avoids turning his head to watch the flight of the ball when it is hit to his partner and instead keys on the opposing net men, watching them, even while his partner hits the ball. While watching the opposing team, he might lose sight of the ball for a brief instant, but he will pick up the sight of it in the periphery of his vision. The movements made by the opponents will give him an early clue as to where his partner hit it, and he can then focus on the ball and react quickly to play it (Figure 67).

If he were to turn his head sideward to watch the ball as his partner hit it, he would have to turn his head again to follow the flight of the ball. He would most likely not see any unexpected moves by the opposition, and might be taken by surprise by these moves.

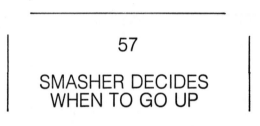

57

SMASHER DECIDES WHEN TO GO UP

Frequently, during the course of an exchange in doubles, a team at the net is forced to smash a deep lob. Both players should retreat in this situation, but often some confusion occurs as to whether they should advance to the net after the smash or stay in their relatively deep positions. A particularly untenable position occurs when one player decides to advance while the other stays back.

Such confusion can be avoided if both players agree beforehand that in such a situation the player who smashes the ball decides whether to go up or to stay back. His partner, watching him closely, reacts accordingly, staying back if the smasher stays back and advancing if the smasher advances (Figure 68).

The smasher should be permitted to make the decision in this situation because he can determine better than his partner can how

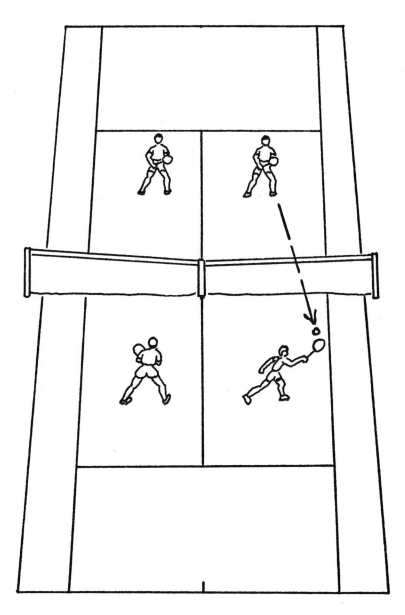

Figure 67

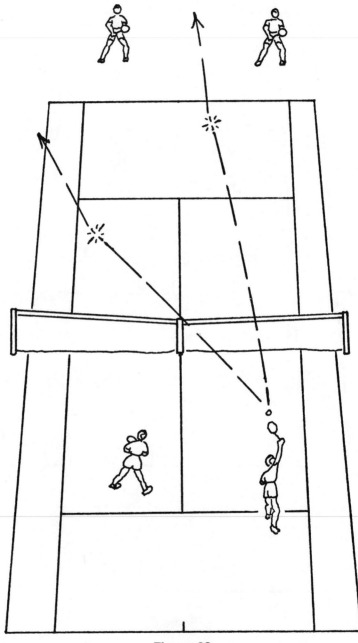

Figure 68

effective his smash will be. Should he misjudge the lob, for instance, and not be able to smash it forcefully, or if he were to decide to let it bounce for any reason, he mostly likely would decide not to advance to the net after playing the ball. His partner, watching him, could then follow his lead and stay back also.

58

MOVE TOWARD THE BALL

The tactical principle of being on the line-of-good-position applies to a doubles team as well as to singles play. Simply stated, for doubles, it is: *players move toward the ball* (Figure 69).

As player A moves wide to his right to play a ball, his partner (B) should move to the right, also, moving toward the ball, to decrease the size of the opening created between the two players.

The opposing players (X and Y) move toward the ball, also. Player X moves to his left to cover a possible hard shot down the alley by A; as he does so, he creates a wide gap between himself and his partner, Y. His partner then also moves to his left to close this gap.

59

TWO SMALL HOLES, NOT ONE BIG ONE

Doubles players should move as a team. As one man moves in one direction to play a ball, his partner should move in the same direction. The idea can best be expressed as "giving them two

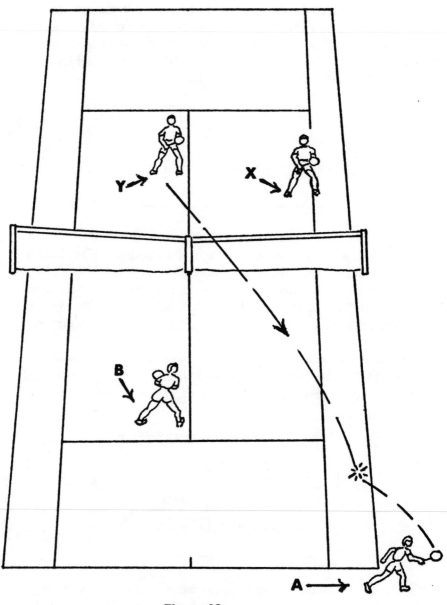

Figure 69

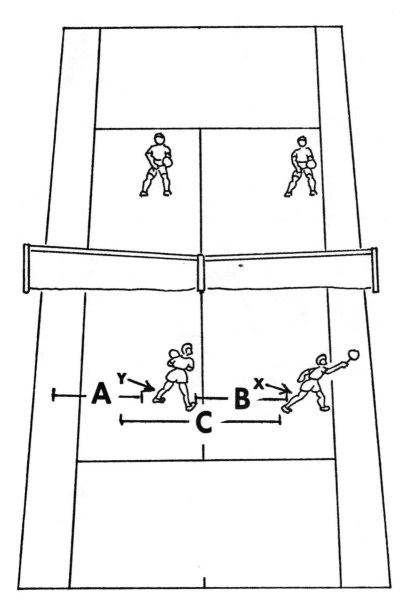

Figure 70

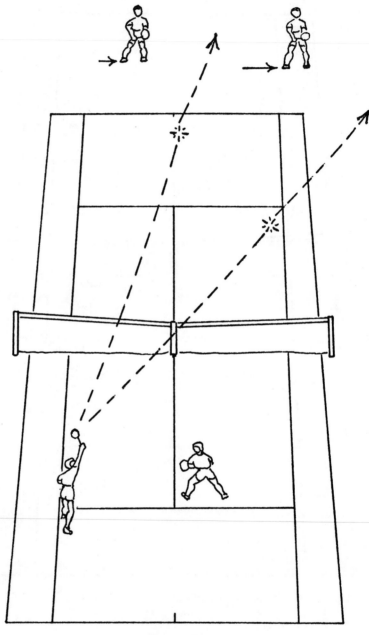

Figure 71

small holes into which to hit rather than one big hole.'' (Figure 70).

As Player X moves to his right to play a ball, he leaves a big opening (C) between himself and his partner (Player Y). Player Y, seeing that his partner must move to the right, knows that this hole is being opened between him and his partner so he quickly moves to his right, also, closing the hole somewhat, but meanwhile opening a hole on his left. He thus creates two small holes (A and B) and closes the big hole (C), reasoning that it is more difficult for the opponents to hit through the small holes than through the big one.

60

COVER THE ANGLES

When a doubles team is deep on the defensive, and is lobbing to the opposing net team, they should anticipate the possible angles of the net men's smashes and act accordingly.

When the smash is being made from the side of the court (Figure 71), the retrieving men should be aware that the smasher can angle the ball quite sharply toward the opposite side of the court. They should move, then, to cover this angle: both men move toward the open side of the court, closing the opening on this side and keeping constant the opening between them. As they move toward the side of the court, they create an opening on the side away from which they move. What they have actually done, however, is to transform two small openings and one big one into three small openings. It will be much easier for them to cover these three small openings than to cover the big opening plus two small ones.

VIII

Drills for Conditioning

Because competitive tennis is a strenuous game, optimum performance in it requires maximum fitness. As important as good strokes and sound tactics are, they alone will not suffice in high level competitive play. They must be augmented by certain other qualities that enable a player to make most effective use of his good strokes and permit him to employ the tactical plan necessary to win the match.

A number of conditioning drills are used by successful coaches and players to develop the qualities that assure maximum performance. These drills are designed to condition players in four general areas: strength, flexibility, agility, and coordination and endurance.

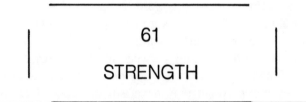

61

STRENGTH

Successful play in tennis does not require that one be a "Charles Atlas" or a "muscle man." What is required, however, is a certain degree of strength in the hitting hand, and in the wrist, the forearm, and, to some degree, in the shoulder muscles of the hitting side of the body.

The drills described below will do much to develop this necessary strength. They should be done regularly throughout the season. The drills tend to "tighten up" a player for a short period of time —recovery is rapid, however—so they are best used following, rather than prior to, practice periods. They should be avoided immediately prior to a match.

COVERED-RACKET WALL RALLYING

Rallying against a wall or backboard with a head-cover on the racket is one of the best and quickest ways for a player to develop strength in the hitting arm. He can hit ground strokes, serves, and volleys, but he should be careful to use his regular grips when doing so.

ROLLING UP A SHEET OF NEWSPAPER

The exercise of rolling up a double page of newspaper with the hitting hand adds immeasurably to grip strength if done regularly. The paper is held at one corner, with the arm outstretched from the body, and the player simply tries to roll it into as small a ball as possible. His hand will become tired in a minute or two, but he will be developing strength for tennis.

FIST-AND-STRETCH

The simple exercise of making a tight fist then stretching the fingers of the hand develops strength in the hitting hand and forearm. A player should do this about 50 times for a few days; then about 75 times for a few days. From then on, he should do it about 100 times two or three times a week.

WRIST-BENDING

A player can develop strength in the wrist by holding a heavy book in his hitting hand, resting his forearm on a table so that his hand and the book hang over the edge of the table (palm down), and then raising and lowering the book by bending his wrist up and down. After about 50 such exercises, he should then turn his forearm so that his palm is up and do 50 more exercises. Doing this two or three times a week will develop and maintain adequate wrist strength.

62

FLEXIBILITY DRILLS

The twisting, bending, leaping, and stretching required in active tennis play demand that a successful player be loose, supple, and flexible in all parts of his body not only for superior performance but to avoid bodily injury, as well.

Several exercises, shown in Figure 72, are effective as a means of conditioning players so that their bodies can respond successfully to the rigorous demands of the game. They should be done regularly throughout the season and are especially effective when used as warm-up procedures prior to play and practice.

63

AGILITY AND COORDINATION

There is no questioning the need for quick, graceful, coordinated movement for successful tennis play. The quick stops and starts, the changing of direction following short dashes about the court, and the quickness in recovering from off-balance and out-of-court positions simply demand that a player be agile and swift.

The exercises illustrated in Figure 73 can do much to improve a

Figure 72

EXERCISES FOR AGILITY

CRAB WALK

REVERSE CRAB WALK

KNEE JUMP

SPREAD JUMP   TOUCH JUMP

BURPEES

JUMP THRU

Figure 73

player's agility and coordination. They should be done regularly throughout the season, also.

64

SPEED AND ENDURANCE

Not often is a tennis player taxed to the limit of his endurance. Only in a long, drawn-out match does endurance become a problem. An ambitious tennis player, however—one aspiring to above-average performance—should be prepared for these long, drawn-out matches. Regular participation in the drills described below can do much to improve endurance and speed.

WHISTLE-STOP

Players spread out in the back court area, staggering their positions so that they are equi-distant from players adjacent to them. A coach or leader stands in front of the group, facing them.

The coach blows a short blast on a whistle and all players immediately start quickly and run forward. After the players have run forward a few steps, the coach blows another short blast on the whistle and the players immediately reverse direction, running backward. The coach continues to blow the whistle at regular intervals as the players respond to each blast of the whistle by running forward and backward, changing direction each time the whistle is blown.

Two or three two-minute running periods, interspersed with 30-second rest periods, is an effective routine. As players become conditioned, however, the duration and number of the running periods should be increased so that they are forced to run near or at the point of exhaustion.

A variation is one in which the players run to the left and to the right, changing direction when the whistle is blown. They should look straight ahead, over the net, as they run.

POINT AND GO

Players spread out in the back court area and stand in the ready position, facing the net. The coach or leader stands in front of them, facing them.

The coach extends either his left or right arm and points, either to the side, forward, backward, or forward or backward at an angle. Players respond to the coach's pointing movement by running in the direction in which the coach points.

The coach lets the players run a few steps, then points in another direction. He makes the players run in all directions, making them change direction quickly. Two or three 3-minute periods of running, interspersed with 30-second rest periods, is a good routine early in the season. The length and number of running periods should be increased as the season progresses and as the players attain greater endurance.

ME-AND-MY-SHADOW

Players are paired off, with each holding a racket in his hitting hand. One member of each pair is designated the leader, the other, the shadow. The leader assumes the ready position, facing the net, somewhere in the back court area. His "shadow" stands three feet behind him, also in the ready position.

The leader then simulates a movement—any movement—he would have to make in actual tennis play. He can pivot and swing for a forehand or a backhand; he can run forward to "play" a short ball, either forehand or backhand; he can run to either side, or obliquely, forward or backward, to "play" a forehand or a backhand. The "shadow" duplicates whatever movement his leader makes. The drill continues with the leader trying to "lose" or confuse his shadow.

After three or four minutes of action, players are given a 15 second rest period and then exchange roles (the leader becomes the shadow, the shadow becomes the leader) as they resume the drill.

MOANIN' LOW

All players line up along a side fence, with their backs to the fence. On a signal to start, they run across the court to the opposite fence, touching every line that they cross on the way, and return to the starting position, again touching every line they cross. Chalk can be used to extend the center line to the baselines so that players positioned in the back court areas must touch this line. Four or five consecutive trips across the court, a 30 second rest, and four or five more trips is a good routine.

A variation is to have them run forward in one direction and backward in the other direction. They touch all lines again as they run.

SPOT-RUNNING

Running in place, or spot-running, is a good conditioner. Players should vary the speed at which they run, changing from slow to fast to slow on command. They should also vary the height to which they raise their knees, moving their feet barely off the ground—moving them as fast as they can—and then bringing their knees very high, trying to touch their chests with them but moving their feet as fast as they can.

IX

Drills and Formations for Beginner's Stroke Instruction

The tennis instructor who conducts group or class instruction in a school or recreation program usually has too many players and too few courts. Frequently, he is instructing a class of from 15-25 students and is faced with the following problems:

1. Selecting formations and class arrangements that make the most effective use of the available facilities.
2. Giving individual attention to each member of the class or group.
3. Providing for individual differences in the development of form, style, and technique.
4. Providing actual play experience for members of a large group when only a few courts are available.

Solutions to these problems are not always apparent to an inexperienced instructor. Experienced instructors, on the other hand, have devised the following answers to these problems:

1. *Selecting formations and class arrangments.*
   The physical arrangements of teaching situations differ. Since each instructor has a unique set-up of courts and related facilities, he must select formations which suit his particular situation. Several formations using one court for a group of 12-20 players are shown in the accompanying

diagrams. These can serve as a guide to an instructor who must devise similar formations that will be applicable to his unique situation.

2. *Giving individual attention.*

By moving around the court (or courts) from player to player, an instructor can provide individual instruction. If the group is large, he is able to spend only a very short time with each player. However, through the use of the "buddy system" an instructor can "multiply himself" and thus provide additional individual attention for his students. This system, in which the students coach each other by working in pairs, requires that the students have a knowledge of specific checkpoints relating to the skills of the game. (A sample of a checkpoint chart or card is shown in Chapter 12).

3. *Providing for individual differences.*

No two players will develop identical styles. As individual differences are noticed, they should be encouraged, provided the general development of form is in accord with what is generally regarded as correct or good form. The concept of a *range of correctness* will provide for the development of these differences. When teaching a skill, the checkpoints mentioned previously should be stressed but slight deviations from them should be permitted if they do not result in flagrant violations of accepted good form.

4. *Providing actual play experience.*

If by play we mean actual full-scale competition in tennis, it may be impossible to provide actual play experience for each member of a large group. Perhaps, the best an instructor can do is to organize and provide drills that are similar to actual competitive play situations.

When there are few courts available, the use of stations can provide some experience for competitive play, even in the case of a large group. Stations can be set up on various parts of one court with forehand drills in one corner, backhand drills in another, serve practice in another, and volley drills in another. Several members of the group can be assigned to each of the stations to work on skills and drills, while other members of the group are assigned to whatever other courts are available for actual play, either singles or doubles. The small groups should be rotated from time to time so that eventually every player is assigned to each of the stations and to a court for actual play.

As an alternative, the instructor can schedule matches between group members (a round-robin tournament, a single or double elimination tournament, etc.) to be played outside of class time on whatever courts are available either at the school or in the community. Instruction and practice occurs during class time, play experience is obtained outside class hours.

65

STROKE AND SWING PRACTICE

The open-order formation is used for stroke and swing practice. The class spreads out on the playing area (Figure 74) so that each member is about eight feet away from the nearest member. Students are asked to extend their rackets at waist level, first in the right hand and then in the left hand, and to swing them around slowly in a complete circle. If any students touch rackets, they are too close to each other; they should then adjust their positions accordingly.

The instructor stands in front of the group, facing the students as he gives explanations. To demonstrate skills or to lead the class through stroke practice, he turns into the sideways-to-the-net hitting position, turning his head to talk to the group over his shoulder. After leading the students through several practice swings, he can walk among them and check each student's swing, and make whatever suggestions and corrections are appropriate.

If detailed demonstration or explanation become necessary, the group can quickly assemble around the instructor in close order formation. Students can then return to their original open order formation for stroke practice. Numbered circles or X's may be chalk drawn on the court surface to facilitate open order formation and roll taking.

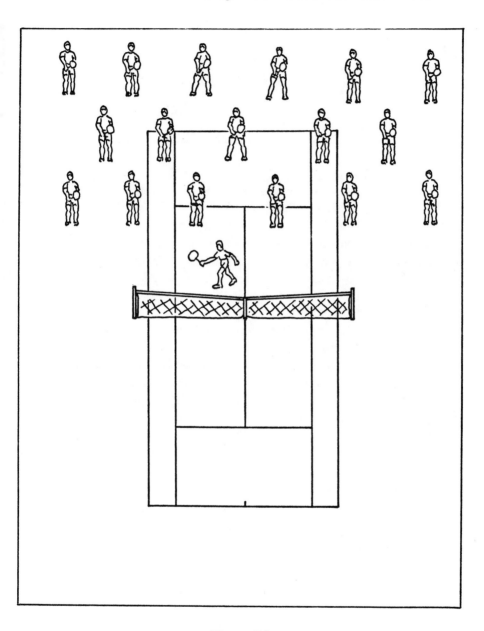

Figure 74

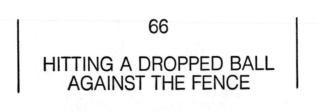

66

HITTING A DROPPED BALL AGAINST THE FENCE

When a majority of class members are ready for advancement, the class should move to the next level of development, hitting a dropped ball. This step is important and necessary because a player will need to drop-and-hit with some degree of accuracy time and time again throughout his tennis career. When warming-up before starting play in a match, for example, both players are expected to feed balls nicely to each other to allow practice hits. Beginning players bounce-and-hit to provide accurate shots in all their practice sessions, too.

The class can be divided into small groups of two's, three's, or four's for initial practice in hitting a dropped ball. Number one's, standing about 10 feet from the fence, can hit first, with number two's acting as buddy coaches while three's and four's act as retrievers who roll the balls back to the hitters (Figure 75). Number one's can drop for themselves and hit, or they can hit a ball dropped by number two's; number three's and four's then could act as coaches and retrievers. Balls can be hit against the side fence or against the end fence. The groups should rotate from time to time so that all players get equal hitting, coaching, and retrieving time.

67

HITTING A DROPPED BALL TO A PARTNER

When hitters have learned to stroke the ball with reasonably good form, they move 30 feet away from the fence and

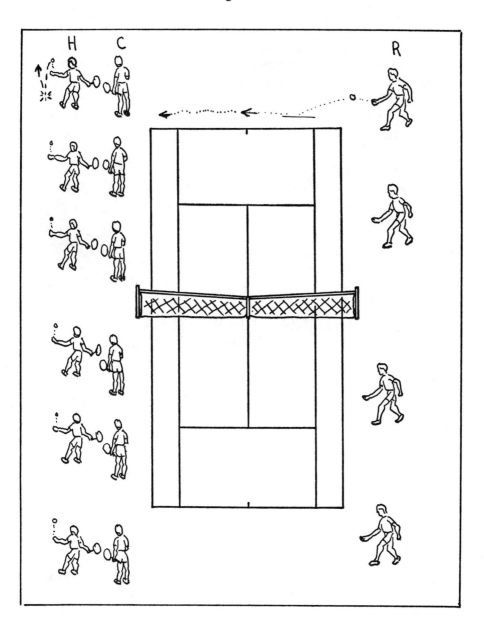

Figure 75

their partners stand directly against the fence, facing the hitters. The hitters then drop-and-hit to their partners, who catch or retrieve balls and return them to the hitters (Figure 76). Emphasis should be on accuracy and control at this point, not on speed. The catchers, against the fence, act as targets, (with hitters trying to hit every ball directly to their targets). Other players act as coaches and retrievers. Positions are rotated regularly so that all players get equal hitting time.

Students can be motivated to stress accuracy by having them compete with each other in a contest to see who can ''hit the target'' most often when making some designated number of successive drop-and-hits.

68

HITTING A DROPPED BALL OVER THE NET

When further skill has been achieved at proper stroking, hitters can drop balls and hit them over the net (Figure 77). For safety reasons, not more than four hitters should be in action at one time.

Hitters are spread along a baseline, with three or four players lined up in file formation behind each hitter. Other players act as retrievers at the net and against the far fence.

Hitters, each with a small bucket of balls (the cardboard buckets obtained free from a famous maker of 31 flavors of ice cream are ideal for this), drop balls and hit them over the net. Retrievers at the far fence roll the balls back to the hitters' side of the court. Balls can be rolled easily and safely if the bottom of the net is unfastened, rolled up part way, and secured at intervals with five-inch length of wire or coat hanger, or with ordinary paper clips, made into S-hooks. Groups are rotated regularly so that all players get equal hitting time.

An advanced dropped-ball drill is one in which hitters stand in

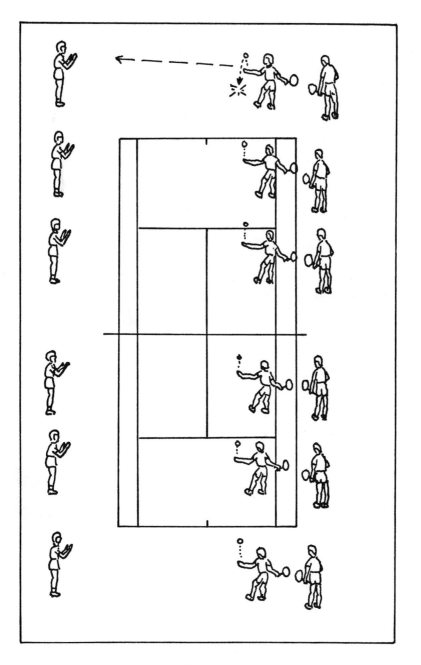

Figure 76

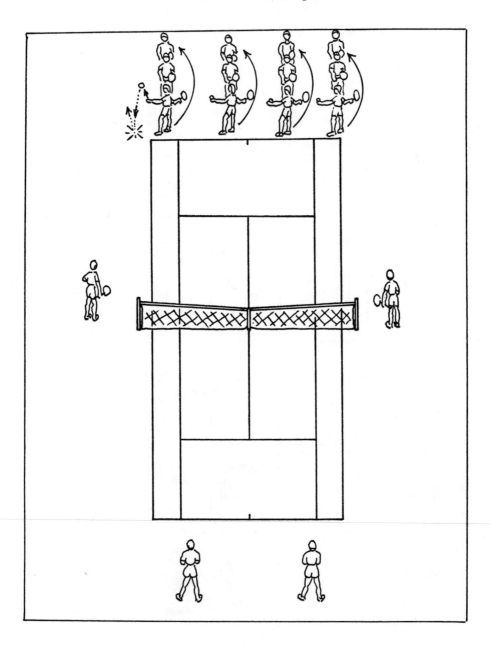

Figure 77

the waiting position and toss the balls a few feet away from themselves so that they must turn and hit, turning from the waiting position to the hitting position (Figure 78). Both forehands and backhands can be practiced as hitters rotate from the front of one file to the end of the other after hitting 8 or 10 balls.

69

HITTING A SHORT TOSS AGAINST THE FENCE

The next step in the development of the stroke—hitting a tossed ball—introduces the hitter to additional problems in stroking: timing his swing to the oncoming ball and stepping properly to reach the ball. The hitter now has to time his backswing, his step, and his forward swing; he must learn to make these moves in the proper sequence and with the proper rhythm that permits a smooth, unhurried swing, and an accurate hit.

Here, as in dropped-ball drills, the hitters swing from a sideways stance, hitting against either the side fence or the end fence. Tossers stand very close to the fence, with their backs to it, and slightly to the right of the hitters (for backhands, tossers would stand to the left of the hitters). Hitters stand about 10 feet away from the tossers (Figure 79).

The tosser tosses the ball underhanded so that it bounces up easily to the hitter's strike zone (a "friendly toss"). The ball will be coming at the hitter at a slight angle, but this will present no problem even for the lowest beginner. As the toss is made, the tosser moves to his left quickly, just a few feet, so that he is in no danger of being struck by an errant hit.

The hitter lets the ball bounce, steps, and swings to hit the ball not at the tosser but directly against the fence.

Using check-points as a guide, the tosser coaches the hitter. Other non-hitters can act as retrievers, and as coaches also. Groups are rotated periodically so that all players get equal hitting practice.

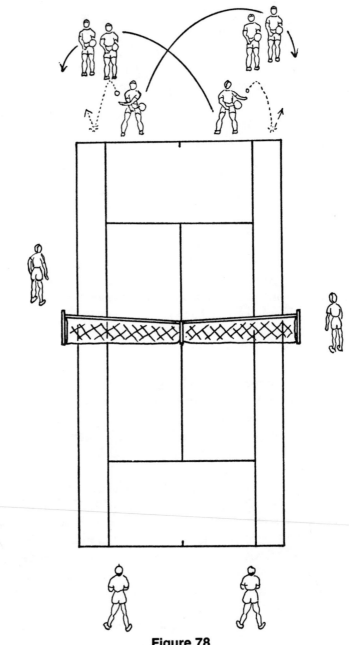

Figure 78

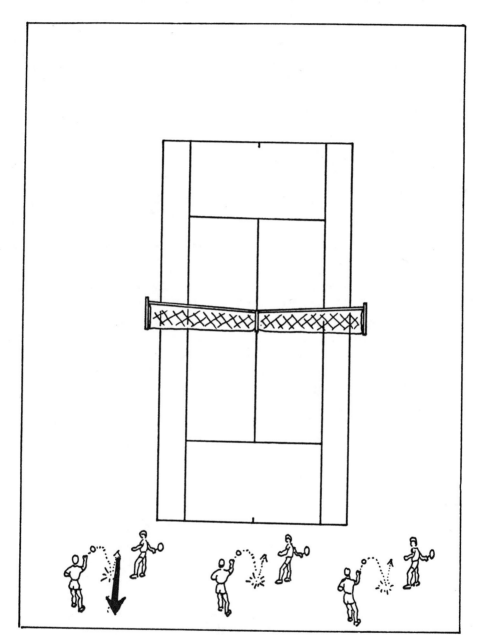

Figure 79

Hitters should be cautioned not to endanger the tossers by hitting wildly and hard. Chalk marks, correctly spaced, assure that both hitters and tossers are sufficiently spread so that no danger is inherent in the drill. Not more than three groups of hitters-tossers should be used at any one section of the court.

70

HITTING A LONG
TOSS TO TOSSER

The class advances from hitting short tosses against the fence to hitting long tosses across the court back to the tossers. The hitter starts from the waiting position (facing the tosser) or from a hitting position (sideways to the tosser). The tosser stands with his back against the fence about 30 feet away from the hitter, and tosses balls so that they bounce up nicely on one hop for the hitter to hit (Figure 80). It is often necessary here to provide targets for the tossers to aim at. Chalk marks or scuff marks on the court surface, in front of each hitter help the tossers to gauge their tosses. Once they learn the proper trajectory of the toss they'll be able to provide convenient bounces for the hitters. A variation of this formation is one in which the hitters stand near the net while the tossers stand near the end fences. The hitters then hit toward the end fences (Figure 81).

Regardless of the formation used, for safety reasons not more than three groups of hitters should be assigned to either end of the court. For safety reasons, hitters should be cautioned against wild, hard hitting.

The coach or instructor can circulate behind the hitters, offering suggestions and tips on stroking. If additional students must be used, they can be assigned to the roll of retrievers or coaches. Groups should be rotated so that all students share hitting time equally.

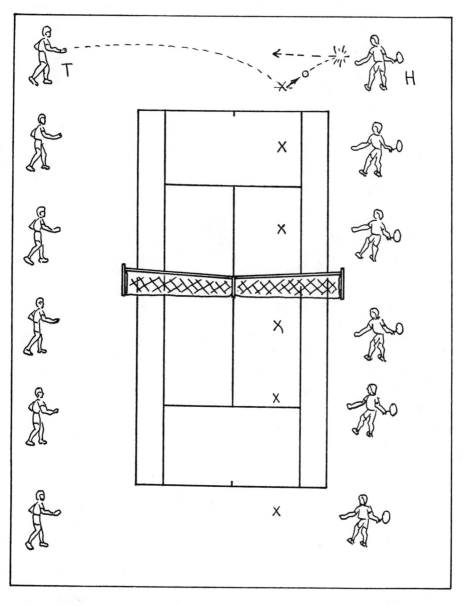

Figure 80

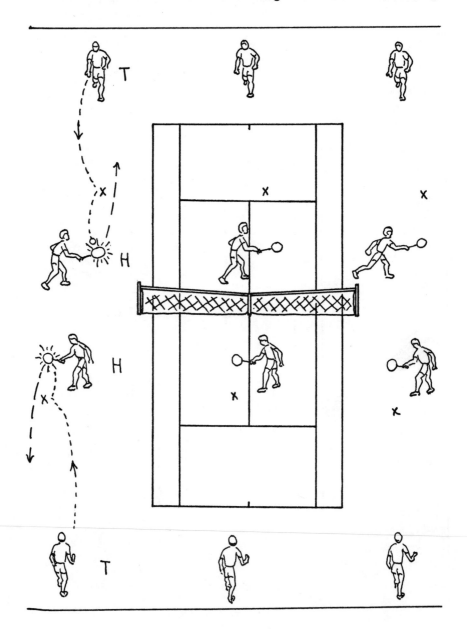

Figure 81

71

HITTING TOSSED BALLS
OVER THE NET

The four-player unit of hitter, coach, tosser, and retriever can be used to give students practice in hitting long tosses
over the net. To minimize the danger of students being struck by
stroke balls, not more than three hitters should be assigned to one
court (Figure 82).

Hitters should be spread along one base line, one in each alley
and one on the center mark. A coach is assigned to each hitter and
stands behind his hitter. For safety reasons, tossers kneel or sit on
the opposite court, close to the net. Retrievers are assigned to the
end fence behind the tossers.

Each hitter tries to hit the ball directly over his tosser's head.
Each tosser tries to set the ball up for his hitter, giving him a
"friendly" toss (chalk or scuff marks can be used as targets for the
tossers). Retrievers return the balls to the tossers by rolling them to
the net.

The instructor moves from group to group, offering suggestions and making corrections, and rotates the groups regularly to
give all students equal hitting time.

If students are very young or are unable to toss accurately, the
instructor can toss to them (Figure 83). Students form two files,
with the instructor standing at the net in the opposite court. He
tosses five or six balls to the first student in each file, after which
these students move to the ends of the files and the next man in the
file becomes the hitter.

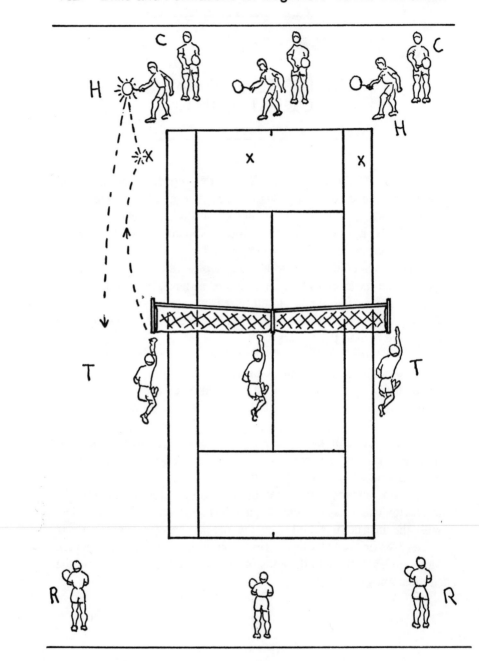

Figure 82

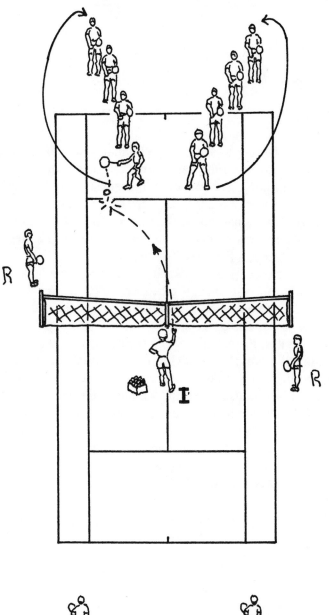

Figure 83

72

STRIKE ZONE

During tossed-ball drills, hitters will experience some practice in moving to the ball, as not all tosses will be made precisely to the hitting area. Whatever movement is required, however, will consist of only a short step or two in whatever direction is necessary. Additional practice in moving to hit a tossed ball, with the tosser deliberately making the hitter move several steps, is the next logical step in the learning sequence.

Inexperienced players usually find deep, high-bouncing balls particularly difficult, though others are difficult, too. It should be explained to them that the easiest ball to play is one that levels off at about the waist. The concept of the baseball strike zone is helpful in explaining this: the batter must hit the ball if it is in the strike zone because it is relatively easy to hit. If it is outside the strike zone (too low, too high, too wide, or too close), he does not have to hit it because it is too difficult to hit. Similarly, the easiest ball to hit in tennis is one that is in the strike zone, and, preferably, levelling off in the middle of it.

High-bouncing balls will travel through the strike zone twice, once on the way up and again on the way down. These balls are most easily played as they fall downward through the strike zone; they have less speed and thus are easier to judge and time.

Low balls can be played in the strike zone if the player lowers his strike zone by bending his knees. For wide balls, the player moves his strike zone (it is attached to his body, so to speak) to where the ball is to play it the easiest way.

Figure 84 illustrates a drill that gives players practice in learning to move their bodies so that they can play most balls in the middle of their strike zones. The group is divided into units of two, with one player acting as tosser and the other as hitter. No rackets are used; hitters merely practice catching the ball at waist level with thei hitting hands. Tossers mix-up their tosses so that the hitters

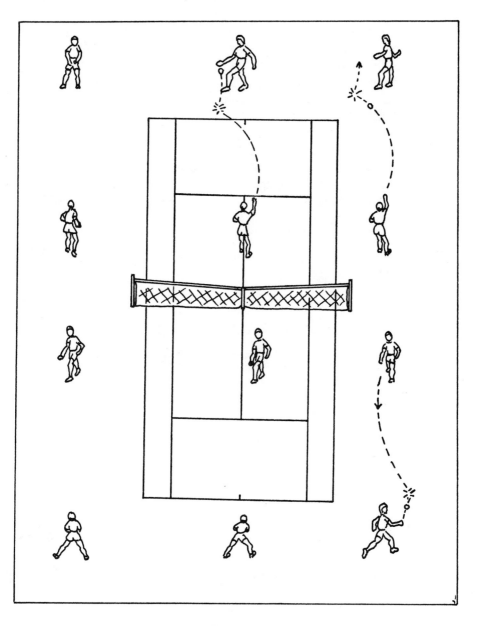

Figure 84

must move their strike zones to where the ball is. Hitters can start from the hitting position, sideways to the tosser, or from the waiting position, facing the tosser. In either case, they hold their hitting elbows very close to their right hips, with the arms bent so that the forearms are parallel to the ground at waist level. They then try to catch the ball in their hitting hands *without moving their arms*. Tossers should mix up their tosses, forcing the hitters to move forward, sideward, and backward, and away from a ball tossed directly at them. After the hitters have learned to catch the ball, they can take very short swings and hit the ball easily with their hands, being careful to play the ball at waist level (in the middle of their strike zones).

Players should be rotated regularly so that all get equal practice in learning to judge the ball so that they can play it in their strike zones.

73

RUNNING TO HIT TOSSED BALLS

Following the strike zone drill, players should be given practice in using the strike zone concept as they run-and-hit the ball.

Court arrangements for this drill (Figure 85) are similar to those used in previous drills. Care must be taken to spread the groups sufficiently to provide ample room for the hitters to move in all directions. It may be necessary to have the hitters take turns at running to hit, after the teacher has first offered mass instruction in moving.

The tossers make the hitters move sideward, backward, and forward, and away from a ball tossed directly at them. Hitters should be encouraged to try to follow the sequence of "run, stop, and hit," hitting with good balance and returning quickly to the starting position ("home base") after each hit.

Players are rotated at regular intervals so that all get equal hitting time. Both forehand and backhand strokes can be practiced.

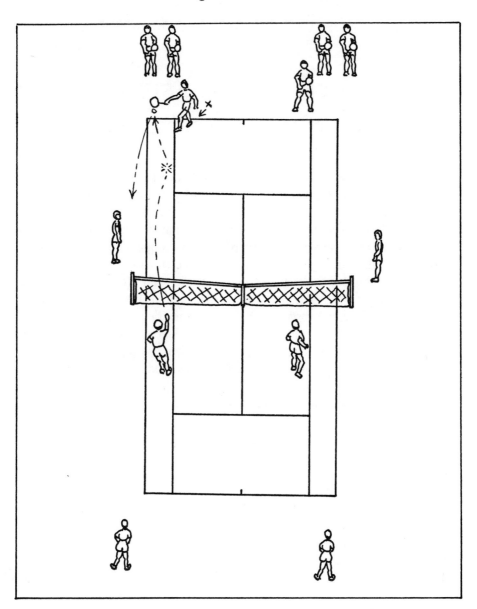

Figure 85

74

CIRCLE GROUND STROKES

A group of players can practice ground strokes on only one court using a drill called Circle Ground Strokes (Figure 86).

Players form two files, one on each end of the court, with the first player in each file about two feet behind the center mark. Either of these players starts a rally by dropping-and-hitting a ground stroke over the net to the first player in the opposite file, who returns the ball with a ground stroke. Each player, after he hits, moves to the end of his file as the second player in each file quickly moves to the front position. These players then drive the ball, each hitting only once, and move to the end of the file as the next player in moves forward to the hitting position. The ball is kept in play, then, as each group rotates after each hit. When any player misses, either of the front players starts a new rally and rotation continues as players try to sustain the rally.

The drill can be restricted to forehands only, backhands only, or to either forehands or backhands. No volleys are permitted; all balls must be played as a ground stroke, on the first bounce, and must land within the singles court.

Fun and friendly competition can be provided by the drill by having a contest: a point is scored against a player each time he misses. After a prescribed time period, the player with the fewest points is the winner.

If two units are working on one court (Double Circle Ground Strokes, Figure 87), or if units on one court are competing against each other on adjacent courts, each unit counts the number of consecutive hits it makes before a miss occurs. After a given time period, the unit that had the longest rally is the winner.

The drill can be made more difficult for intermediate players by restricting the area into which they can hit to the back court—the area bounded by the baseline and the service line. It can be made even more difficult for advanced players through the addition of

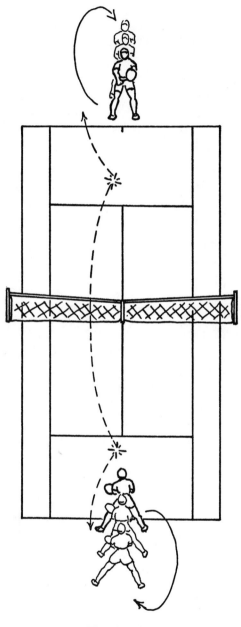

Figure 86

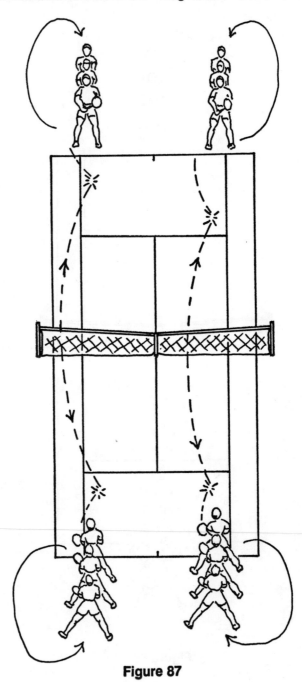

Figure 87

deep lines drawn across the end of each court, about eight feet inside each baseline; balls must then land inside the deep area to be considered good.

75

PLACING THE GROUND STROKES

Even beginning players, after only a short period of practice in hitting, become concerned about being able to "place" the ball. They want to learn how to hit it not only straight ahead ("down the line") but at an angle ("cross-court") as well.

Placing the ball involves subtleties in timing and in changing the forearm-wrist-racket angle. Players can be given practice in learning to apply these subtle changes in stroke technique by having them deliberately hit balls that come to them at an angle. Working in groups of three's, two players act as tossers while one acts as the hitter. With the hitters hitting away from the net, toward the rear fences, 12 players can be accommodated safely on one court (Figure 88).

Tossers alternate their tosses as the hitters try to place balls to either of the tossers.

Players are rotated frequently so that all get equal hitting time. Both forehands and backhands can be practiced in this manner. The units can consist of four players, also, with the fourth man acting as a coach for the hitter.

Players can be given practice in placing their ground-strokes by returning balls fed to them by the coach (Figure 89). Hitters line up in two files, with a file near the junction of the baseline and each singles side lines. The coach, or feeder, stands in the center of the opposite baseline. He drops-and-feeds balls to the first hitter in one file who practices placing his shots either straight ahead or cross-court as called for by the coach. After eight or nine feeds (no rallies) the hitter moves to the end of his file and the man next in line moves forward to the hitting position. The coach then feeds the first man in

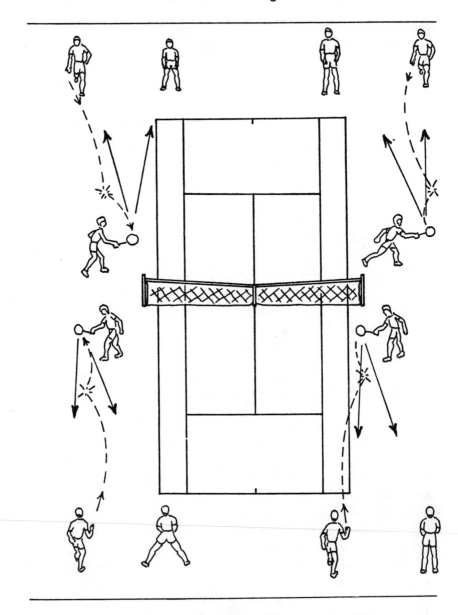

Figure 88

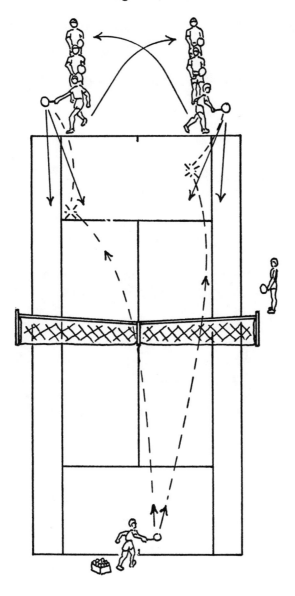

Figure 89

the other file. After eight or nine hits, the coach feeds the front man in the first file as men in the second file change positions.

Players not in files act as retrievers. Groups are rotated period-ically so that all players get hitting practice.

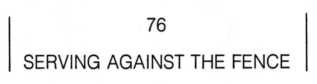

76

SERVING AGAINST THE FENCE

For serving instruction, pupils are placed on the court exactly as they were for swing drills, for here too, they will first make "dummy" swings before actually hitting a ball. They should be spread out on the court so that each has sufficient room to swing freely.

Practice in the swing follows a clear and concise explanation and demonstration of the serve. First teach them to trace the proper racket path. When the swing is learned, shift emphasis to the toss, telling hitters how to hold the ball and how to toss it. For practice at this have them first combine the swing with a "fake" toss. When the proper rhythm is learned (when they can synchronize the move-ment of the arms) have them toss a "live" ball. And lastly, have them toss a ball and actually hit it.

For hitting practice, first have the group serve toward a fence to encourage concentration on the stroke rather than on the result. The group lines up about 15 feet from the fence (Figure 90, A) and each player serves against the fence. If the group is large and fence space is limited, half the group practices the serve while the other half retrieves, each retriever standing behind a hitter. If the class is conducted on a court (or on more than one court) there will almost certainly be enough fence space to allow everyone to hit at the same time. Hitters can be spread around the entire fence area, standing about 15 feet from the fence and spaced about nine feet apart. The teacher moves from hitter to hitter, making suggestions and correc-tions as he does so. After a short time, retrievers become hitters and hitters become retrievers.

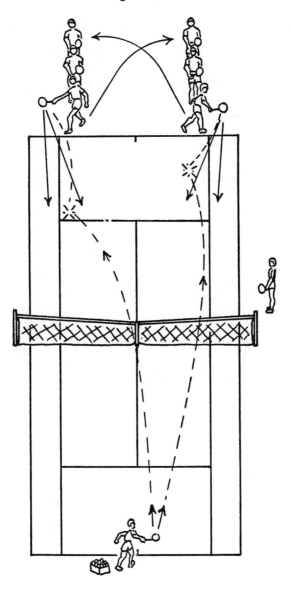

Figure 89

the other file. After eight or nine hits, the coach feeds the front man in the first file as men in the second file change positions.

Players not in files act as retrievers. Groups are rotated periodically so that all players get hitting practice.

76

SERVING AGAINST THE FENCE

For serving instruction, pupils are placed on the court exactly as they were for swing drills, for here too, they will first make "dummy" swings before actually hitting a ball. They should be spread out on the court so that each has sufficient room to swing freely.

Practice in the swing follows a clear and concise explanation and demonstration of the serve. First teach them to trace the proper racket path. When the swing is learned, shift emphasis to the toss, telling hitters how to hold the ball and how to toss it. For practice at this have them first combine the swing with a "fake" toss. When the proper rhythm is learned (when they can synchronize the movement of the arms) have them toss a "live" ball. And lastly, have them toss a ball and actually hit it.

For hitting practice, first have the group serve toward a fence to encourage concentration on the stroke rather than on the result. The group lines up about 15 feet from the fence (Figure 90, A) and each player serves against the fence. If the group is large and fence space is limited, half the group practices the serve while the other half retrieves, each retriever standing behind a hitter. If the class is conducted on a court (or on more than one court) there will almost certainly be enough fence space to allow everyone to hit at the same time. Hitters can be spread around the entire fence area, standing about 15 feet from the fence and spaced about nine feet apart. The teacher moves from hitter to hitter, making suggestions and corrections as he does so. After a short time, retrievers become hitters and hitters become retrievers.

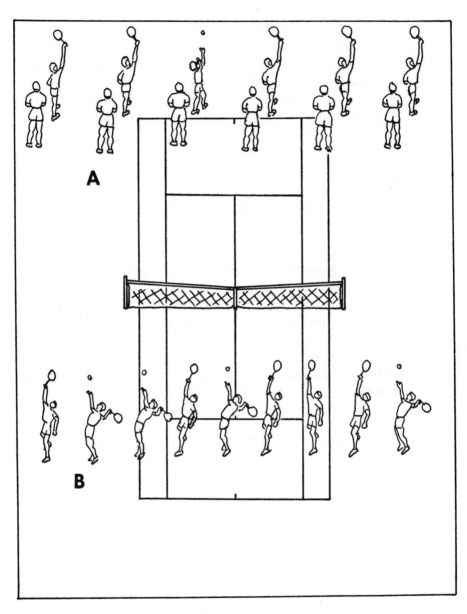

Figure 90

An advancement of this drill is one in which the hitters stand about 30 feet from the fence (near a service line) and serve against the fence (Figure 90, B). Not all balls that are hit will roll back to the servers; many will come to rest close to the fence. Care should be taken, then, to see that all players retrieve balls at the same time so that no one is serving while others are retrieving.

77

SERVING OVER THE NET

When the majority of the class can execute a reasonably good serving motion, the entire class should be given realistic serving practice on the court.

Six players can serve simultaneously from one baseline while another six retrieve balls against the far fence. After each of the servers serves five or six balls, the balls are collected by the players who are standing against the fence. These players then move up to their baseline and serve five or six balls each; the previous servers move back against the fence and become retrievers, collecting the balls (Figure 91).

Players are rotated from right of the center mark to left of the center mark so that they practice serving in both the left and right courts.

The teacher stations himself near the servers and makes corrections in their swings as he moves along the serving line.

Additional class members can be assigned to be retrievers, standing to the side of the net until balls are to be retrieved. They can be rotated into the serving line also.

Slow learners and poorly coordinated players are grouped together and permitted to serve from a service line, or from various points between the service line and the baseline. As they develop control they are gradually moved back to the baseline.

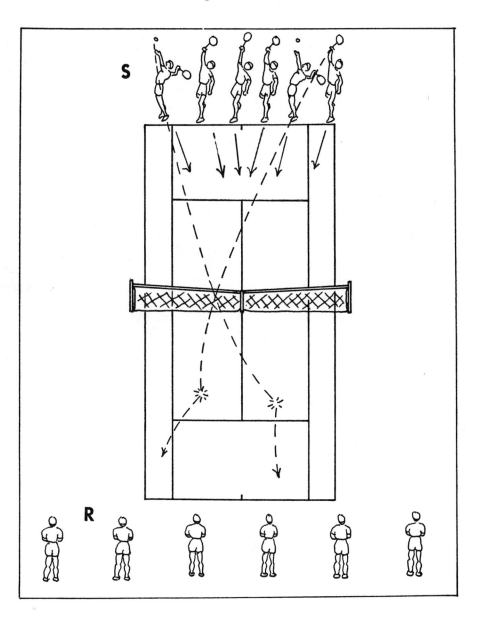

Figure 91

78

COMBINED SERVES
AND RETURN OF SERVES

Serving practice can be combined with return-of-serve practice by having half the group act as servers while the other half acts as receivers. Half the serving group starts from the right of the center mark, half starts from the left. Similarly, half the receiving group starts in the right court, half in the left. The first person in each line plays five or six balls (five or six serves or five or six returns), after which he moves to the end of the opposite line. The second person in each line moves into the serving position then (or the receiving position), serves (or receives) five or six times, and then moves to the end of the opposite line. In this manner, players get practice in serving (or receiving) in both the left and right courts (Figure 92).

For safety reasons, the serves should stagger their hits so that two players are not serving at exactly the same time.

After all players on the serving side have served five or six balls (or more, depending upon the number of balls available), all balls are retrieved by all players and the players reverse positions: receivers become servers, servers become receivers.

Both serving positions and receiving positions can be varied so that all players get serving and receiving practice for both singles and doubles play.

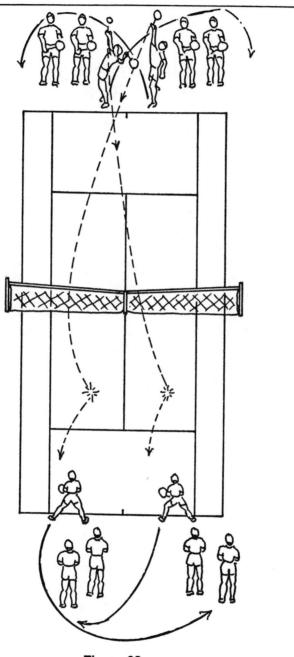

Figure 92

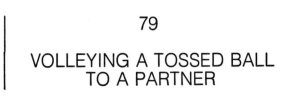

79

VOLLEYING A TOSSED BALL
TO A PARTNER

An effective means of introducing players to the technique of volleying the ball is to have each player play "patty cake" with another player for a few minutes. Players pair off and stand about a foot from their partners, in a slightly sideways-to-each-other position. Each player extends his hitting hand, with his arm bent slightly, and "pats" his hand against his partner's hand. A few minutes of "patty cake" practice gives players the feel of the short, jabbing stroke used in the volley.

Next, players spread out a little so that the distance between partners is about 8-10 feet and simply play one-handed catch with each other, tossing underhand and catching with the hitting hand. This is done either crosswise on the court, with players throwing toward the sidelines (Figure 93, A), or lengthwise, with players throwing toward the net and rear fence (Figure 93, B). For convenience in retrieving balls one line of players is placed about six feet from a fence. Their partners stand about 20 feet from them, each pair spaced about 10 feet from any other.

After partners have played catch for a few minutes, one player of each pair uses his racket to volley balls tossed by his partner. Players reverse the procedure on command of the teacher: tossers become hitters and hitters become tossers. All of this is done in the original line-up, either sideways across the court or lengthwise toward the net and rear fence with hitters hitting toward the fence.

Tossers are asked to make friendly tosses, tossing underhand and merely setting the ball up for the hitter. Hitters merely block the ball with their rackets or jab it back to the tosser lightly.

Forehand volleys, backhand volleys, and a mixture of forehands and backhands can be practiced in either of these formations. The teacher or coach moves from unit to unit as he offers

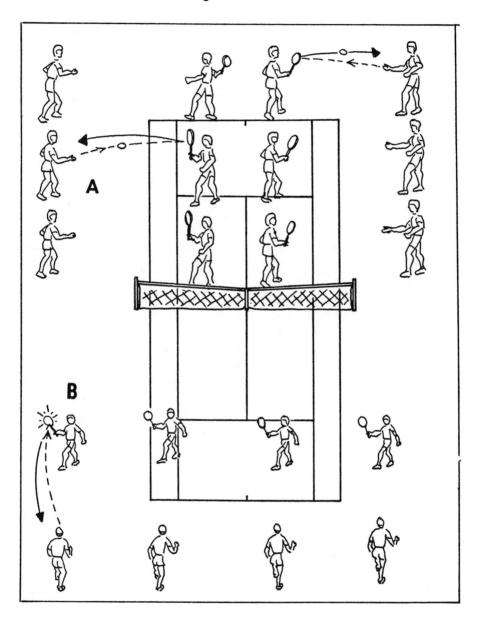

Figure 93

suggestions and makes corrections. Additional students can be assigned to stand behind the hitters to act as coaches or to be ball retrievers. Assignments should be rotated regularly.

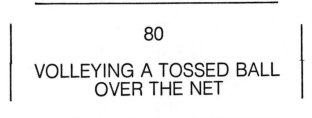

80

VOLLEYING A TOSSED BALL OVER THE NET

After pupils have had some practice in volleying tossed balls to their partners, they are ready to learn to volley over the net. The four player unit of coach, hitter, tosser, and retriever can be used, with two units working on one court at the same time. Players not involved in the two active units serve as retrievers stationed around the court (Figure 94).

Two hitters take positions in the standard volleying position, about eight feet from the net, each about six feet from a singles side line. Tossers sit on the court directly opposite the hitters, on the other side of the net, sitting very close to the net so that the net serves as a protective screen for them. Waiting players stand behind each hitter and act as coaches for the hitters, while other players act as retrievers, rolling the balls back to the tossers.

Tossers "feed" balls to the volleyers by tossing to them. Volleyers volley over the tossers' heads. Forehands, backhands, and a mixture of forehands and backhands can be practiced.

The coach stands near the volleyers to offer coaching tips and cues, and rotates the groups regularly so that all get equal volleying time.

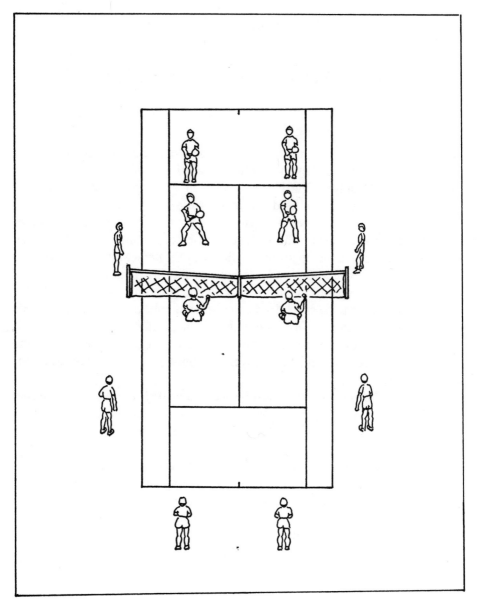

Figure 94

81

VOLLEYING A DRIVEN BALL

Several drills can be used to give players practice in the next step in volleying—volleying a driven ball.

If only a few players make up a group, the drill shown in Figure 95 can be used. Players form a file on one side of the net, with the first player in the file in the normal volleying position, eight to nine feet from the net astride the center line. The coach takes position on the opposite baseline near the center mark, and acts as a feeder as he drops-and-hits balls to the first man in the volleyer's file, giving him forehands only and then backhands only. The ball is not rallied; the coach feeds, the net man volleys, and the coach feeds again. After the first man in the file has volleyed for a few minutes, he moves to the end of the file as the second man moves up and becomes the volleyer. Players continue to rotate as the drill continues.

If more players must be accommodated, players form two files in the volleying positions, one on the forehand side and the other on the backhand side of the court (Figure 96). The coach feeds forehand volleys to the first man on the forehand side; then backhand volleys to the first man on the backhand side; then forehand volleys to the second man on the forehand side, and so on, as players in each file rotate from front to back. Files exchange places from time to time, also, so that all players practice both forehand and backhand volleys.

In either drill, the coach should have a box or basket full of balls at his disposal. When all balls have been hit, all players retrieve them, refilling the basket or box, and the drill is resumed.

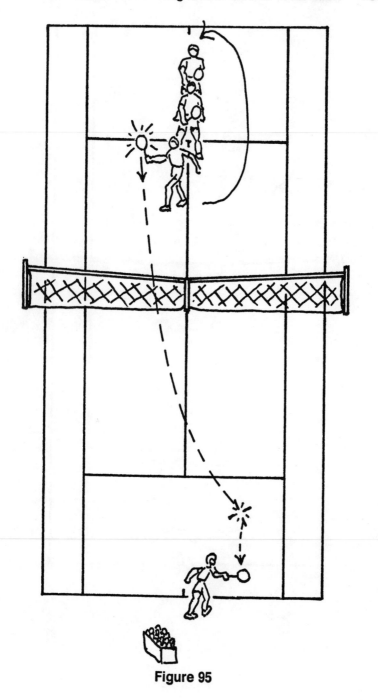

Figure 95

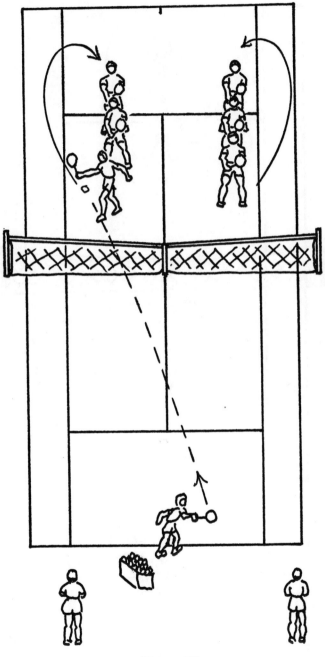

Figure 96

82

ROPE VOLLEYING

A variation of the volleying drill is one in which a rope is strung across each end of the court, about 10 feet from the end fences. Volleyers can stand between the end fences and the rope, which simulates a net, while drivers stand near the net and drive toward the volleyers (Figure 97). One court, then, is converted to two half-courts, and twice as many players can be accommodated in the drill.

Streamers (cloth, string, or tape) are hung from the rope at intervals to make the rope more visible, and short elastic "shock-cord" is attached to each end of it to lessen the possibility of injury should a player inadvertently run into it. Small S-hooks, attached to the shock-cord, enable one to attach the rope to fences very easily. If there are no side fences to which the S-hooks can be attached, fairly heavy objects such as a chair, a weighted vertical post, etc. can be used for attaching purposes.

Volleyers and drivers attempt to rally with each other. Players are rotated so that each gets volleying practice and driving practice.

83

A COACH AND FIVE

Players can combine volleying practice with ground stroke practice in a drill called A Coach and Five (Figure 98).

Three players take positions in the back court, with one player behind the center mark and each of the other two behind a singles sideline. Two players take normal doubles volleying positions at the net. The coach, with an ample supply of balls placed near him,

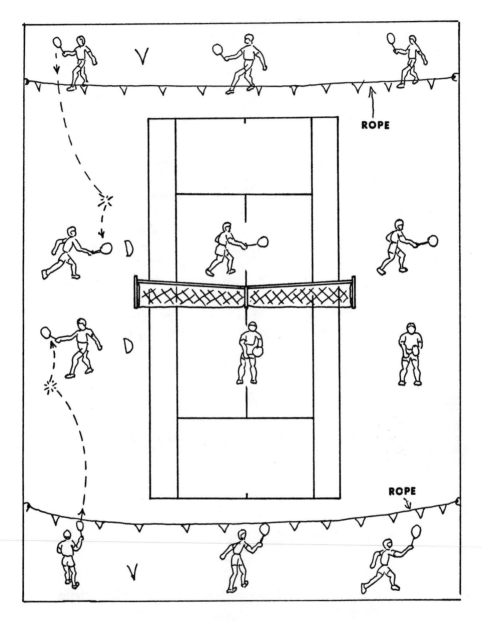

Figure 97

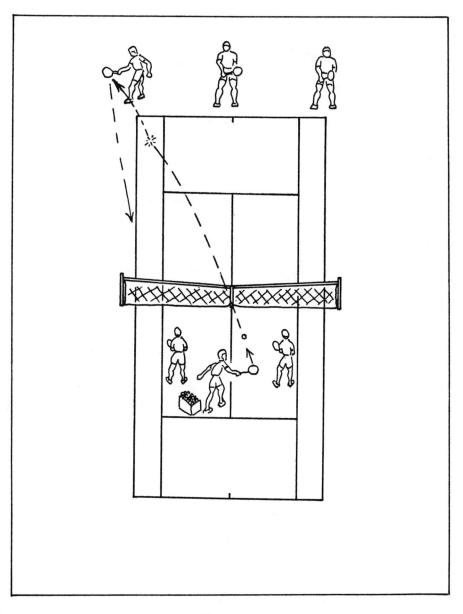

Figure 98

stands behind the volleyers at the junction of the center line and the service line.

The coach drops-and-hits a ball to one of the backcourt players who drives the ball back at either of the volleyers. All players try to sustain the rally. When a ball is missed, the coach quickly drops-and-feeds another ball, and another rally takes place.

Players are rotated periodically so that they all get practice in all positions on the court. Additional group members can act as retrievers, stationed around the court, and can be rotated into the hitting groups periodically.

84

CIRCLE GROUND STROKES AND VOLLEYS

The basic Circle Ground Stroke drill can be used to provide practice in volleys and ground strokes.

Players form two files, one at the net, the other in the opposite back court (Figure 99). The first player in either file starts a rally with the first player in the opposite file. Each player hits the ball only once, then quickly moves to the rear of his file; other players in each file move forward while the ball is in play. The front player in each file tries to return the ball that comes to him as he moves to the front position: one player volleys, the other hits a ground stroke. All players try to keep the rally going as long as possible. When a ball is missed, another rally is started.

Two units can be engaged in the same drill, with one unit on each side of the court (Figure 100). Players should then be careful to rotate to the outside, toward the sidelines, to avoid bumping into each other. Units can compete against each other in a contest to see which unit can have the longest rally. Each unit keeps its own count, counting out loud. At the end of the prescribed time period, a "longest rally" winner can be declared.

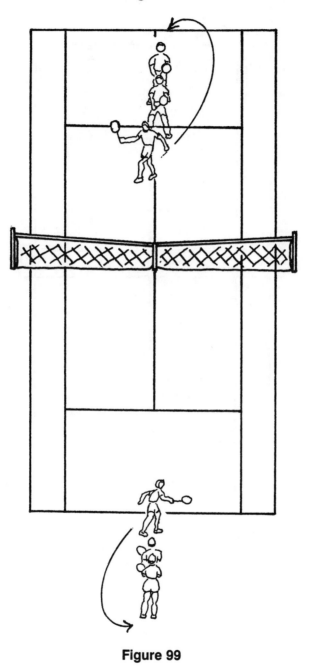

Figure 99

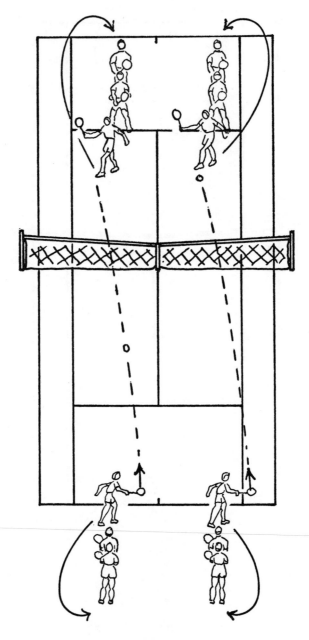

Figure 100

85

LOBBING A TOSSED BALL

The tosser-hitter-retriever unit can be used to introduce players to the lob: one player tosses, one lobs, one retrieves. Three units can work safely on one court (Figure 101).

The lobbers stand about three feet behind the baseline, one behind each singles sideline and one behind the center mark. Tossers take positions at the far side of the net, close to it, opposite their hitting partners. The remaining players act as retrievers, or, standing behind the lobbers, as coaches.

Tosses are made to land near target-marks (X's) drawn close to the baseline. The hitters lob the ball back over the tosser's heads, trying to make the ball land deep in the opposite court. Tossers can toss to the lobber's forehands only, to their backhands only, or to both forehands and backhands.

Groups are rotated frequently so that all players get equal lobbing practice.

86

LOBBING A DRIVEN BALL

Players are given practice in lobbing a driven ball by having feeders drop-and-hit to them (Figure 102).

Three hitters spread out on the baseline. Two players stand in the opposite court, in the normal net positions. One member of the class stands between the net-men on about the service line to act as a feeder to the lobbers. He drops-and-hits, driving the ball to each lobber alternately. Lobbers try to lob balls over the net-men so that

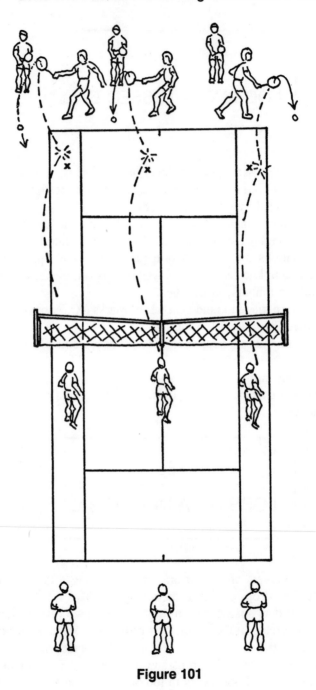

Figure 101

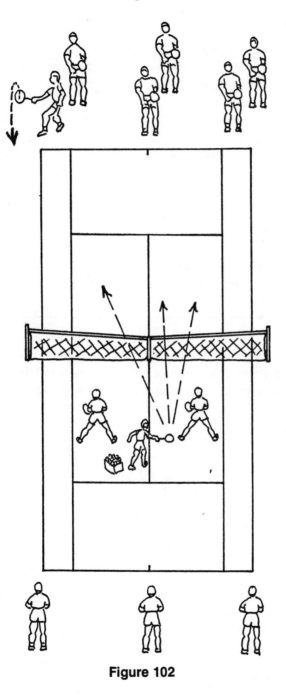

Figure 102

the lobs land deep in the court. The net-men *do not* return the lobs, even if they can reach them; they merely act as targets for the lobbers to lob over. Other players act as retrievers stationed around the court returning balls to the feeder. Lobbers are given both forehands and backhands.

The feeder moves to the baseline after all lobbers have acquired some "feel" for the shot and feeds from deep in the court.

Groups are rotated regularly to give each player lobbing practice.

87

SMASHING TOSSED BALLS AGAINST THE FENCE

The overhead smash, if practiced carelessly, can result in injury to a player unfortunate enough to be struck by a hard hit ball. This is especially true when beginners, who cannot control the speed or direction of their smashes, are first introduced to the stroke in a group stiuation.

The danger of injury can be avoided if fleece balls (cotton balls), sock balls (old socks stuffed with paper and bound with tape), or paper balls (newspaper rolled into the shape of a tennis ball and bound with tape) are used in hitter-tosser drills. Tossers stand against either the side fence or the end fence, and toss lobs to smashers who stand 20-30 feet away from the fence (Figure 103). Smashers smash the tossed ball back at the tosser; because the ball is soft, no danger results from errant or misdirected hits.

Eight players, (four tossers, four smashers) can be accommodated easily and safely on any one section of the court (Figure 103).

Players are rotated regularly so that all get equal hitting time. The teacher or coach moves along the line of smashers offering suggestions and teaching cues.

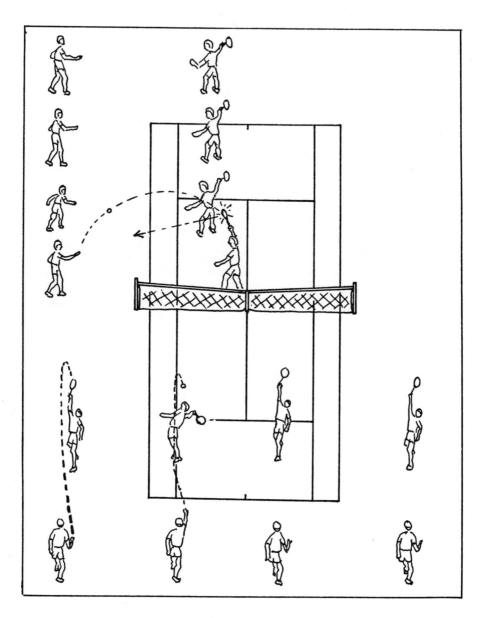

Figure 103

88

SMASHING TOSSED BALLS OVER THE NET

Players can be introduced to smashing over the net by having them hit tossed balls. Tossers sit on the court, very close to the net, and toss to smashers; the net protects the tossers from hard, errant smashes (Figure 104).

The smash is an enervating stroke, one that players should not practice for too long a time during any one practice period. For this reason, several players can be on the smasher's side of the net. Each smasher then makes only eight or nine smashes before moving off court to let another player become the smasher. Other members of the group act as retrievers, rolling balls against the net to the tossers. Players are rotated regularly so that all get equal smashing time. Tossers should stagger their tosses so that both smashers are not smashing at the same time.

89

FULL COURT SMASHING

The final step in introducing players to the overhead smash is to have them smash a drop-and-hit and a lobbed ball.

The drill is similar to the previous one (Figure 104), but the ball is fed to the smasher by a drop-and-hit rather than by a toss, with the feeder starting midway between the baseline and the service line (Figure 105, A). By dropping-and-hitting, he lobs to the smasher, who smashes the ball back. Two units can work at one time on a court if feeders are careful to stagger their feeds so that the smashers are not smashing at the same time.

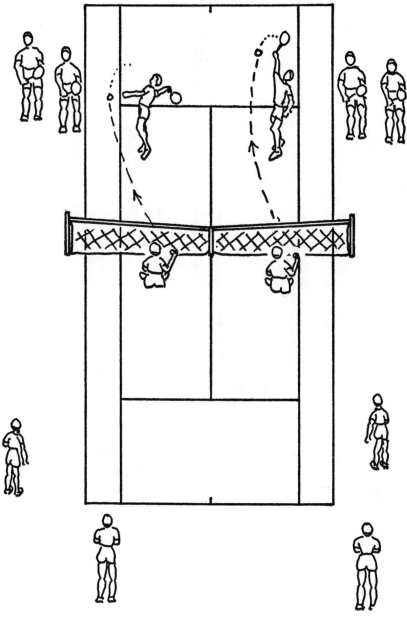

Figure 104

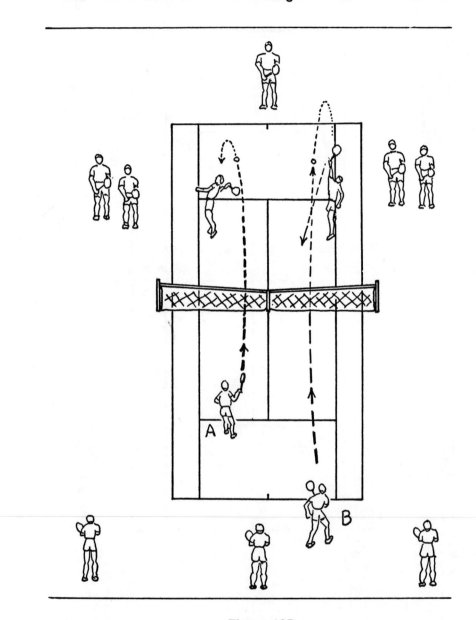

Figure 105

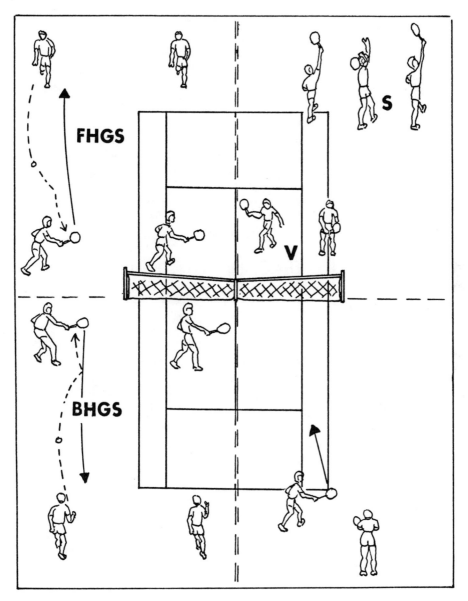

Figure 106

When all players have learned to control the direction of their smashes fairly well, the feeder moves back to just behind the baseline (Figure 105, B) and feeds from this position. If the smasher smashes successfully to the feeder, the feeder lobs the ball back to the smasher. Again, two units can work on one court at the same time.

Players not smashing can wait on the side of the court, adjacent to the smashers, and move into the smashing position when their turns arise (each smasher hits only six or seven balls). Other members of the group can act as retrievers. Rotate the group regularly.

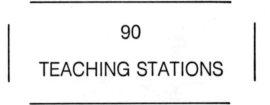

90

TEACHING STATIONS

The court can be divided into four teaching stations to give various players practice on specific strokes (Figure 106). One group of players (those who need the practice) can work on forehand ground strokes tossed-ball drills in one corner of the court. Another group, those weak on backhands, can work on backhand drills in another corner of the court, while a third group can practice serves against the fence in still another corner. Volleys can be practiced in the remaining corner of the court.

The coach or teacher can move from corner to corner, offering teaching cues and making suggestions to the hitters. The groups can be rotated from station to station periodically so that they practice all four strokes.

If other courts are available, additional class members can be assigned to them for actual play (singles or doubles). All players are then rotated regularly, moving through each teaching station and on to a court for play.

X

Modified Games for Class and Group Play

Beginning students should be permitted to engage in actual competitive play as early as possible. They should be taught the basic rules of the game no matter how they play their ground strokes.

Few, if any students in a group or class aspire to become nationally ranked players. Most of them are enrolled in the program merely to learn enough about stroking, tactics, and the rules to enjoy the game as a leisure-time activity. They want to have fun *playing* tennis, and are therefore reluctant to spend hour after hour in tedious stroke practice; they would much prefer to play the game, despite being fully aware that their strokes and tactics might offend purists who are sticklers for correct detail.

A successful teacher, then, plans his teaching program so that students can play after they have had only three or four periods of instruction. He lets them play usually at the close of the class period, perhaps only for a few minutes during the first few class meetings, augmenting the teaching-drill phase of the period with a shorter "play" phase. During subsequent meetings, as the students' skills increase, he gradually shortens the drill phase and lengthens the play phase so that toward the end of the program perhaps only one-quarter of a period is spent on drills and with the remaining three-quarters being used for supervised play. During all play periods much teaching can be done.

Errors in tactics and strategy, of faulty position play, and of stroke execution can be pointed out to students, discussed briefly and perhaps even corrected "on the spot" while play is interrupted briefly. Students become more conscious of deficiencies in their techniques when these techniques are exposed to actual game conditions, too, and are more apt to work on correcting these deficiencies during following drill periods.

In a class or group situation, however, the number of students vs. the number of courts usually precludes any possibility of true game experience. Most often there simply aren't sufficient courts to permit every class member to play regulation singles or doubles. Ingenious teachers have learned that modified games, however, are as effective as regulation games in providing fun for students and in providing an element of competition for them. Several such modified games are presented in the following pages.

91

TRIPLES

Quite often an entire class can engage in actual play on whatever courts are available by having them play Triples (Figure 107).

Three players make up a team, opposing another team made up of three players. Both teams use the two back, one-up formation.

If players A, B, and C are opposing players X, Y, and Z, Player A would serve the first game. Player B plays in the backcourt along with A. Player C plays at the net as he would do in regular doubles, moving from side to side as A serves.

On the receiving team, X receives in the right court; Y in the left court; and Z plays at the net. Z moves from side to side after every point so that the server has an unobstructed lane for serving.

Players on each team rotate positions in a clockwise direction only *after* their team has served. Player X would serve the second game, serving the first point to Player C who, after rotating clock-

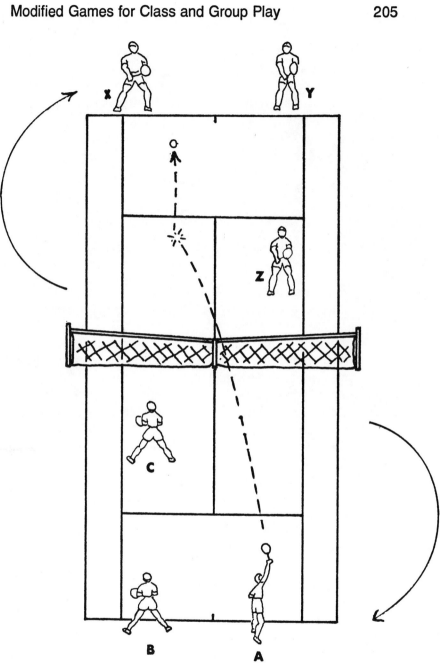

Figure 107

wise after his partner A had served a complete game, would be in the right court to receive the serve.

Player C would serve the third game serving the first point to Player Z, who, having moved clockwise after his partner X had served, would be receiving in the right court.

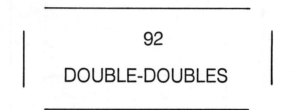

92

DOUBLE-DOUBLES

The game of Double-Doubles (Figure 108), can be used to accommodate a large group of inexperienced players on only a few courts.

Four players on one team oppose four players on another team, using regular tennis rules except that each player serves only every ninth game as the serve is rotated from team to team and from player to player. One player serves an entire game, moving from right to left to right for each point as he would normally do in conventional play (his back-court teammate moves from side to side, also). When serve "goes over" to another team, that team rotates clockwise (with each player moving one position) before serving.

The net men on the receiving team move into the alley while the serve and return are being made, then quickly move into normal volley positions after the return of the serve.

To avoid danger to the net men, they are permitted to play a little deeper than the normal net positions. They are cautioned to look back and watch the ball as their deep teammates play it, too, so that they can avoid being struck by the ball.

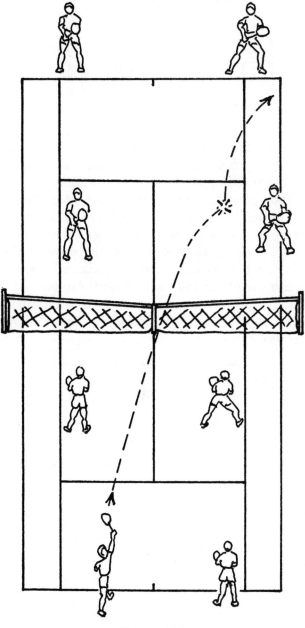

Figure 108

93

DROP-OUT DOUBLES

An entire class of twelve pupils can be introduced to doubles play on only one court by having them play Drop-Out Doubles (Figure 109). Two players start as a team against two other players. They play standard doubles while other class members spread out around the court to act as linesmen and retrievers. When a point is lost by a team, the player who last hit the ball on that team drops out and is replaced by one of the waiting players on his side of the net. With a little experience at this game, all players learn to move in and out of the court quickly and play proceeds rapidly. Players not engaged in actual play must be aware of the score constantly so as not to delay play when they "move in" to replace the player who drops out.

94

AROUND THE WORLD

A simple game which involves hitting for control is illustrated in Figure 110. Two files of players are formed, one on each side of the net. The first man in each file stands on the baseline.

The first player in one of the files drops-and-feeds a ball to the first player in the opposite file. The original feeder then runs around the net post and joins the opposite file. Each player, after he hits, runs to the opposite court to join the file on that court. Players try to "keep the rally going," seeing how long they can keep the ball in play before someone misses. Counting their consecutive hits aloud,

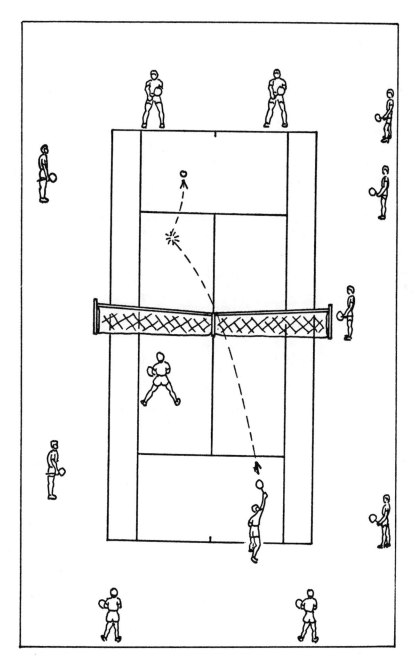

Figure 109

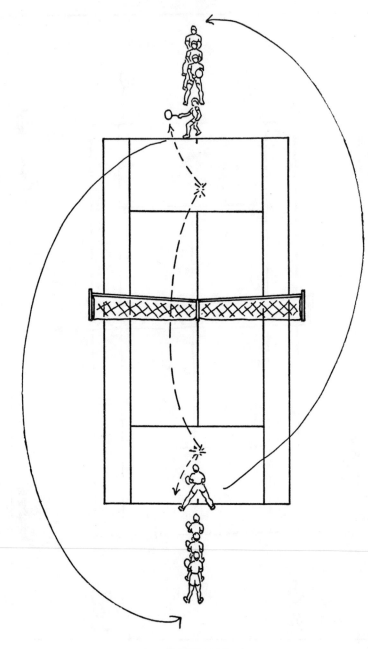

Figure 110

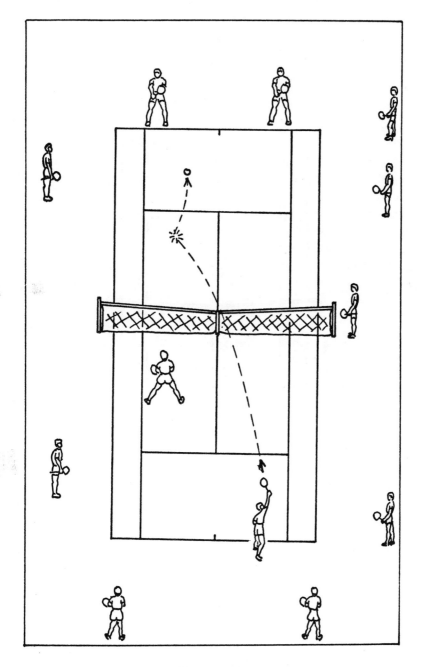

Figure 109

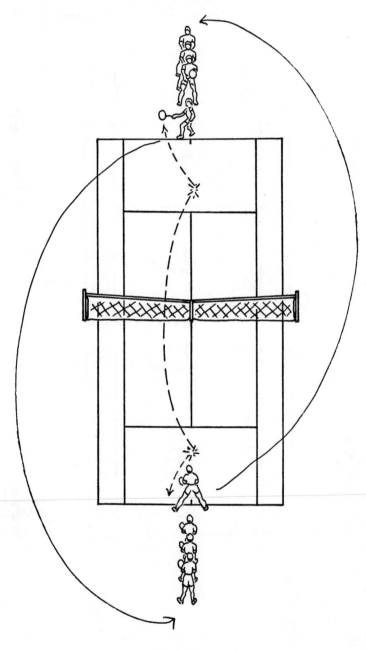

Figure 110

they can compete with another group of players who are playing Around the World on an adjacent court, seeing which group can have the longest rally within a specified time period.

Variations include the following:

1. A point is scored against a player who misses. The player with the least number of points at the end of the time period is the winner.
2. A player drops out when he misses. When only 4 players remain, a new game is started. (Not as effective as No. 1, because the player who most needs the practice is usually the one to miss first.)
3. All hits must land between the service line and the baseline. A ball landing outside this area is a miss.

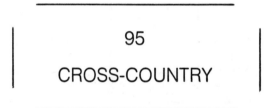

95

CROSS-COUNTRY

Several variations of the game of Cross-Country are used to add fun, competition, and variety to group and class work, especially when young inexperienced players are involved.

The group is divided into two teams of equal size which compete with each other to see which team can first "hit" its way "across the country." Each team "starts" in New York and advances westward to Philadelphia, then on to Pittsburgh, Cleveland, Detroit, Chicago, St. Louis, Denver, Salt Lake City, and finally, San Francisco. A team advances from one city to another when one of its members makes a successful hit to a designated target.

CROSS-COUNTRY GROUND STROKES (FIGURE 111)

Teams line up in file formation on the baseline. The teacher or coach takes a position near the net or on the opposite service line

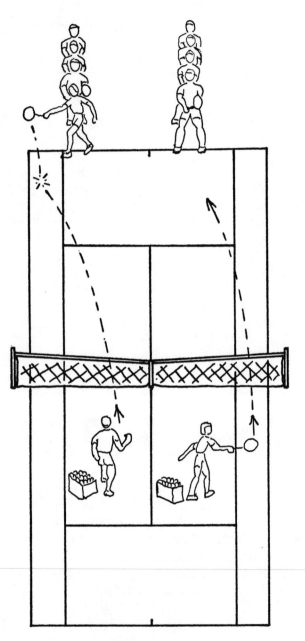

Figure 111

and has available two or three dozen balls. He feeds four balls in a row, using either a toss or a drop-and-hit, to the first player on Team A who tries to hit each ball directly back to the coach. If the coach can touch a stroked ball with either hand without moving his feet, the hitter is considered to have made a successful shot and his team advances to the next city. After four hits, the hitter moves to the end of his file and the next man on the team moves into the hitting position.

The coach or an assistant then feeds four balls to the first man on Team B who tries to advance his team by hitting the ball to the target. Balls are fed alternately then to each team, with each hitter being fed four balls, until one team has advanced to San Francisco.

The degree of difficulty can be varied by using bigger or smaller targets (squares or circles drawn on the court surface in chalk or water-based tempera paint) and by varying the coach-feeder's position to increase or decrease the length of his feed. The game can consist of forehands only, backhands only, or a combination of forehands and backhands. Teams should be given an equal number of hits before a winner is declared.

A chart, made of poster-board, listing the cities in order of advancement and placed at the net or at the side of the court so that it can be seen easily by all players, can serve as a "map" and help each team remember how far it has advanced.

CROSS-COUNTRY SERVES (FIGURE 112)

The serve can be used to play Cross-Country, also. Players serve six balls, each in turn, to a designated target area.

CROSS-COUNTRY VOLLEYS (FIGURE 113)

Cross-Country Volleys is similar to Cross-Country Ground Strokes except that all players volley (either forehands, backhands, or a mixture of the two) to the designated target.

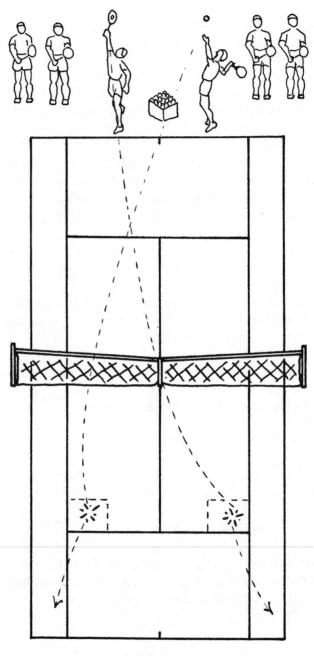

Figure 112

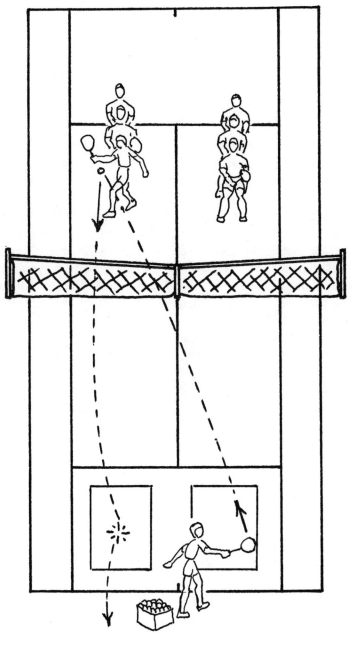

Figure 113

96

TENNIS BASEBALL

There are several versions of Tennis Baseball that successful teachers use to add fun and variety to a program in which very young, inexperienced players are involved. One version, shown in Figure 114, involves eight players.

The class is divided equally into two teams, with one team chosen to bat first while the other fields. The teacher acts as the feeder (the pitcher); his location on the court varies depending upon the skill of the players. He stands close to the net if the players are of very low skill; on the service line if they are more skillful; or back on the baseline if, in his judgment, the players are sufficiently skilled to handle balls fed from there.

The court is marked with chalk or tempera paint as indicated in the diagram. The feeder "pitches" to the batter by dropping-and-hitting (or by tossing) so that his feed lands in the home-plate square (HP in the diagram). If the feed does land in the square, the hitter is required to hit it over the net. A ball hit into the net or beyond the sidelines or baseline is an "out," and the next batter moves into the hitting position. Balls hit successfully over the net into the playing area are scored as to where they land. Each batter stays at bat until he makes an out. All "runners" advance one base for a single, two bases for a double, etc.. After three outs, teams quickly change sides and the fielding team becomes the batting team.

A variation is one in which an out is scored if any member of the feeding team catches a "batted" ball before it bounces twice, regardless of where the ball lands in the court. Hitters are thus encouraged to place the ball away from the fielders, who can play anywhere on the court they desire but who must let each batted ball bounce before trying to catch it, and to try to hit the ball hard so that fielders have difficulty catching it.

Still another variation is one in which the ball is rallied back and forth by the batter and the fielding team. Four players are

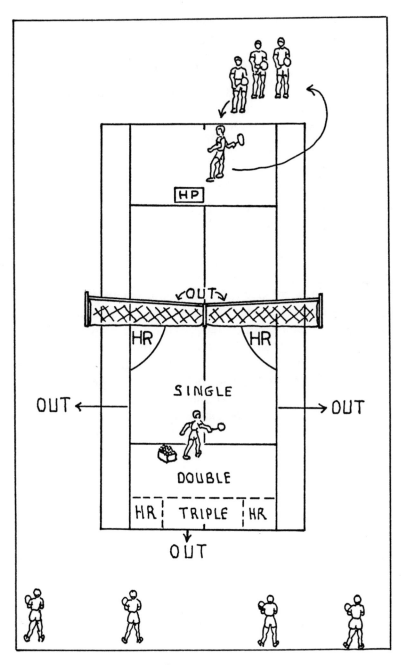

Figure 114

assigned to the fielding team, two at the net and two in the back court. They rally the batted ball back to the hitter's side of the net, and the point is played to its completion. If the batter loses the point, he is "out" and a new batter takes his place. If the batter wins the point, he is awarded a hit determined by where his last shot—the one that was not successfully returned by the fielding team—landed in the fielder's court. He remains at bat until he makes an out.

97

THREE-MAN SINGLES

In a group or class situation where players far outnumber courts, singles play can be modified in order to give every group member experience in actual singles competition.

One such modification is the game of Three-Man Singles in which three players play singles on one court (Figure 115). Players A and B oppose player X, with A and B alternating serves as they play as a team. Player A serves and plays the first point, while B stands off court; B serves and plays the second point while A stands off court. Player A plays the third point, B plays the fourth, and so on, until the completion of the game. Player X, of course, receives all serves.

Player B serves and plays the first point in the second game, Player A serves and plays the second point. B and A alternate playing points until that game is completed. Players then rotate, with A changing places with X. Players B and X then play two games against Player A. When two more games are completed, Player B then changes places with Player A and again two games are played, after which players rotate once more.

In this manner, 3, 6, 9, 12, or 15 players can be actively engaged in regular singles play on 1, 2, 3, 4, or 5 courts, respectively.

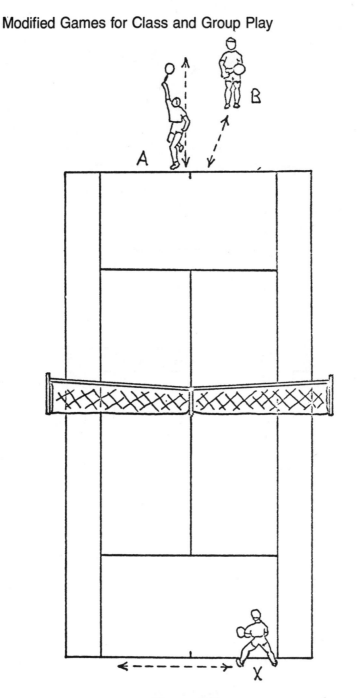

Figure 115

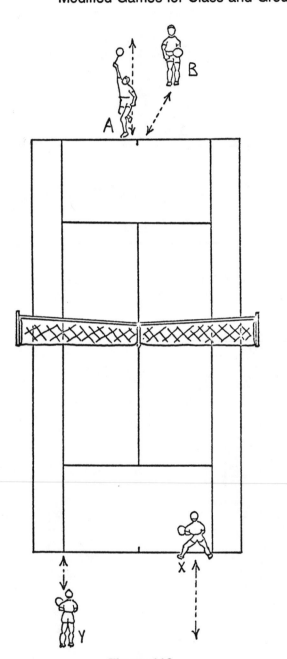

Figure 116

98

FOUR-MAN SINGLES

A large group can be engaged in actual singles play by assigning four players to a court and having them play Four-Man Singles (Figure 116).

The game is similar to Three-Man Singles except that two players make up a team. Players A and B oppose Players X and Y. Players A and B play alternate points during the first game, with A serving from the right and B serving from the left. Players X and Y play alternate points as they receive the serve; X receives in the right court, Y receives in the left court.

Players X and Y then serve the second game as they play alternate points; X plays the first point, Y plays the second, and so on. A and B play alternate points as they receive serve.

Service alternates from team to team after each game, but as it does so after the first two games, the players on the team about to serve exchange positions. If A served the 1st, 3rd, and 5th points (from the right court) during the first game, he would serve the 2nd, 4th, and 6th points (from the left court) during the 3rd game. Similarly, players exchange positions to receive serve. If X received the 1st, 3rd, and 5th points during the first game, he would receive the 2nd, 4th, and 6th points during the 3rd game.

In this manner, 4, 8, or 12 players can play *singles* on 1, 2, or 3 courts, respectively.

XI

An Outline For Teaching Beginning Tennis

I. Introducing students to the game
   A. Explain the idea of the game; use a diagram drawn on floor, court, or blackboard; use a movie (if possible); use star-performers to play a short (1 or 2 games) exhibition.
   B. Demonstrate the basic strokes (forehand and backhand ground strokes, the serve, the volleys, the lob, the overhead smash) by hitting tossed-balls (or have a star performer hit balls tossed by you).
   C. Classify group into smaller homogeneous groups of 2, 3, or 4 members (depending upon class size and number of courts) through use of the *Juggle Test*.

Juggle Test. Using any grip and turning the racket-face over each time to hit balls with both sides of the racket, alternately, a player volleys ("juggles") the ball to himself. Each hit counts one. When a player misses he quickly starts another ball and continues the count. Score = total number of hits during a 1 minute time period. Allow a 15 second practice after a brief explanation and demonstration of the test. Entire group can be tested at one time if enough rackets and balls are available.

Divide class into small groups of 2, 3, or 4 each on the basis of Juggle Test scores; top four scores are one group; next top four scores are another, etc..

222

II. Handling Groups
    A.   Simple mimetic swing drills.
        1. Group spreads out on floor or court, keeping 8-10 feet apart. Left handers on right side of group when group is working on FH, to the left when group works on BH.
        2. Instructor stands in front of group, facing them, to give instructions. He faces in the same direction as group (talks to them over his shoulder) to demonstrate and lead them through swing practice.
        3. Instructor walks among group to make corrections in their swings as they practice the swing.
        4. Players check each other's swing (buddy coaching).
    B.   Hitting drills—dropped or tossed balls.
        1. Group works individually or in pairs, three's, or four's, depending upon group size and space.
Example: No. 1's hit, No. 2's coach or toss; No. 1's hit, No. 2's coach or toss, No. 3's retrieve; No. 1's hit, No. 2's coach, No. 3's toss, No. 4's retrieve.
Rotate positions frequently and regularly so that all players get equal hitting time.
           a. Players hit toward a wall or fence.
           b. On a court, players hit from sideline to sideline, or from net to fence, or from baseline over net.
        2. Instructor walks from hitter to hitter to give individual attention.
        3. Instructor "multiplies himself" by asking players to coach each other (they use check-point chart or card).

III. Steps in teaching the strokes
    A.   Points of form for all strokes.
        1. The grip.
        2. The stance (waiting stance and hitting stance).
        3. The backswing.
        4. The forward swing.
    B.   Levels of development of the ground strokes.
        1. The swing.
        2. Hitting a dropped ball (self-drop or buddy drop).
        3. Hitting a tossed ball.

        4. Running to hit a tossed ball.
        5. Rallying.

IV. Teaching the serve
    A. Points of form.
        1. The grip.
        2. The stance.
        3. The backswing and toss.
        4. The forward swing.
    B. Levels of development.
        1. The swing.
        2. Hit against fence.
        3. Hit over net.

V. Teaching the volleys
    A. Points of form.
        1. The grip.
        2. The stance (waiting and hitting positions).
        3. The backswing.
        4. The forward swing.
    B. Levels of development.
        1. Hit tossed ball to tosser 12' away.
          a.) Tosser throws to target racket.
          b.) Tosser tosses "around the clock."
        2. Volley a drop-and-feed: feeder on service line, then on baseline.
        3. Two-on-one (or 3-on-1) volleying.

VI. Teaching the rules and scoring
    A. Explain the idea of the game, using a diagram drawn on a blackboard or on the court.
    B. Explain the sequence in scoring, using the diagram.
    C. Introduce basic rules by "playing" a game on the diagram.
    D. Have students play mini-hand-tennis on a miniature court (2 paces long, 1 pace wide; 2 rackets placed handle-end to handle-end serve as a net) drawn on floor.
    E. Instructor moves from "court" to "court" to observe, make corrections, and answer questions.

     F.   Students play full scale toss tennis on court.

     G.   Students play regulation tennis.

VII. General class progression

     A.   Progress from one level to next when majority of the class is ready for advancement. Simply test to prove readiness (hit 7 out of 10 to tosser or target, with good form).

     B.   Give Juggle Test after every 4 or 5 lessons and reassign students on basis of the scores to keep small groups homogeneous.

     C.   Let group rally early (to learn timing, judgment, and court position).

     D.   Start with FHGS, but teach BHGS and S early, then teach all three together (while one player serves, others can practice FH and BH by returning the serve).

     E.   Start the volleys and simple overhead smash early so they can play doubles.

     F.   Teach scoring early, so group can actually *play* early.

     G.   If players are small and young (7-10 yrs. old), let them serve underhand, or from 6-8 feet inside baseline.

     H.   Start doubles tactics early.

XII

Check-points for the Basic Strokes

A. *Forehand Ground Stroke*
1. *Grip*: with racket-face edge down, shake hands with the handle, with the 1st finger spread slightly ("short trigger finger"), thumb against side of middle finger, finger-nails of last 3 fingers facing the net.
2. *Waiting stance*: like baseball fielder; left hand at racket's throat, right hand gripping handle properly. Racket pointed toward left net post, at about waist-level.
3. *Hitting stance*: sideways like baseball batter.
4. *Backswing*: Back and up. Racket-face edge down, slight bend in arm, firm grip.
5. *Forward swing*: step with front foot (raise right heel, drag right toe); swing forward and "through the ball." Keep wrist firm after ball-contact; "hit the ball for a long time."
6. *Finish position*: Reach for the left net post, hitting arm fairly straight, racket-head about head-high and edge down, firm grip. "Pose for a picture." "See the butt of the racket."

B. *Backhand Ground Stroke*
1. *Waiting stance*: same as for forehand. Change from FH to BH grip as ball approaches you. *Grip*: with racket-face edge down, put first knuckle almost on top of handle; spread first finger slightly, wrap fingers around handle,

thumb against side of middle finger, fingernails of last 3 fingers on narrow plane of handle.
2. *Hitting stance*: sideways, like left-handed batter.
3. *Backswing*: straight back to "hand on left hip"; racket edge down or slightly open "Hide your hand"; bend arm slightly, elbow fairly close to body.
4. *Forward swing*: step toward ball with front foot (raise left heel, drag left toe). Swing forward and slightly upward and "thru the ball." Keep wrist firm.
5. *Finish position*: Reach toward right net post; racket edge down, wrist chest-high, racket-face head high; firm grip. "Pose for a picture." Forearm blocks out the butt of the racket.

C. *The Serve* ("one, two, a-n-d hit!")
1. *Grip*: forehand grip, but feel that the racket is held more in the fingers. Firm grip, but loose, wobbly wrist.
2. *Stance*: stand like a thrower; line across toes pointing to target, front foot pointing at right net post, rear foot parallel to base line. Aim and sight toward target; rest ball against racket-throat.
3. *Downswing*: arms go down together, left palm facing up, right palm facing down. Arms separate ("spread your wings," "stretch a long rubber band"). Weight back on rear foot.
4. *Upswing*: racket is swung up and toward top of rear fence. (1st knuckle up). "Palm down; elbow back and shoulder-high."
5. *Toss*: push the ball up in line with right net post. Toss about as high as you can reach with top edge of racket. (Tossing palm up).
6. *Forward swing*: keep right elbow high and back. Shift weight to front foot, then drop racket low behind your back ("scratch your back"), and swing racket up and into ball. Hit with a straight arm.
7. *Complete swing*: "one (arms down); two (arms up); a-n-d (ball is going up, racket is poised behind right shoulder);
Hit!" or
"down, up, and hit!"

D. *The Volleys*
1. *Grip*: Same as used for ground strokes (if possible). For quick exchanges: mid-way between FH and BH ground stroke grip.
2. *Stance*: Sideways, if possible. Step forward, or lean forward as hit is made.
3. *Backswing*: Short swing; racket brought back only about 3′ behind point-of-impact. Wrist and grip kept firm. Very little shoulder turn needed.
4. *Forward Swing*: Jab the ball with the racket-head. Keep wrist firm. Jab with the forearm. Very little shoulder turn needed. Jab high volleys down, with little or no backspin. Hit low volleys up easily, either flat or with backspin. "Drag" the racket-face downward, across the ball, to impart backspin. Fast drive—short swing; slow drive—long swing. Backhand volley similar to karate jab. Try to keep racket-face looking at opponent.

E *The Overhead Smash*
1. *Grip*: Same as serve.
2. *Stance*: Same as serve. Get into position below the descending ball, using short quick steps. (Outfielder catching fly ball in baseball.)
3. *Swing*: Similar to serve, except with a shorter backswing. Wait for ball with racket about half-way back.
Swing up and into ball as when serving. Use short follow through.